To commemorate the 750th anniversary of Magna Carta, the American Council of Learned Societies asked four of the world's most noted experts on the subject to discuss its meaning over the years. This volume will be the first in many years to examine Magna Carta in terms which will be of interest both to professional scholars and to the general reader. Considered by some to be a central document of the Western tradition and by others to be largely of mythic importance, Magna Carta has nonetheless played a key role in the legal tradition both of the West and of the countries colonized by the West. These four essays discuss every aspect of this role. Samuel E. Thorne, Professor of Legal History at Harvard, presents Magna Carta's meaning at the time at which it was written, in an essay which may prove to be the classic description. Philip B. Kurland, Professor of Law at the University of Chicago, describes Magna Carta's influence in American law, stressing its relevance to many contemporary controversies on the interpretation of the Constitution. William H. Dunham, Jr., George Burton Adams Professor of History at Yale, discusses the use of Magna Carta in the development of British constitutional law through the eighteenth century, while

(continue

volume contains the Articles as well as the complete Latin Carta, with an English trans

D1161384

THE GREAT CHARTER

PANTHEON BOOKS
A Division of Random House
New York

The Great Charter

FOUR ESSAYS ON MAGNA CARTA
AND THE HISTORY OF OUR LIBERTY

Samuel E. Thorne ⟨ *William H. Dunham, Jr.,*

Philip B. Kurland ⟨ *Sir Ivor Jennings*

WITH AN INTRODUCTION BY *Erwin N. Griswold*

CONTENTS

INTRODUCTION   vii
Dean Erwin N. Griswold, Harvard Law School

I. WHAT MAGNA CARTA WAS   3
Samuel E. Thorne, Professor of Legal
History, Harvard University

II. MAGNA CARTA AND BRITISH
CONSTITUTIONALISM   20
William H. Dunham, Jr., George Burton Adams
Professor of History, Yale University

III. MAGNA CARTA AND CONSTITUTIONALISM
IN THE UNITED STATES: "THE NOBLE
LIE"   48
Philip B. Kurland, Professor of Law,
University of Chicago

IV. MAGNA CARTA AND CONSTITUTIONALISM
IN THE COMMONWEALTH   75
Sir Ivor Jennings, K.B.E., Q.C.,
Master of Trinity Hall, Cambridge University

APPENDIX

THE ARTICLES OF THE BARONS   101

MAGNA CARTA   111

INTRODUCTION

In 1957, the American Bar Association met in London. One of the events of the program was the dedication of a monument at Runnymede. An English barrister was puzzled about this. He asked, "Why are the Americans making such a fuss at Runnymede?" He was told that the lawyers of the United States had erected a monument there in recognition of Magna Carta. He replied, "An interesting historical event, but it had no permanent significance."

But history, like the law, has many fictions. Indeed one can say that history, like the law, is to a considerable extent built on fictions. Plymouth Rock, the Boston Massacre, George Washington, States' Rights—all of these, and many more, have much reality and validity. But all have had a significance in our history above and beyond their own substance, because of the overlay of fiction which has come to accompany them. In a very real sense, the fiction becomes real, and has a significance of its own. Though Jeremy Bentham, with characteristic restraint, referred to "the pestilential breath of fiction," and said that fictions were "the most pernicious and basest sort of lying," * it is clear that fictions—by which, in this context, I mean some form of historical exaggeration—have played an important role at many stages in the development of history.

Perhaps the clearest and most significant example of this process is found in Magna Carta. The importance of Magna Carta is schoolboy learning. Solemn references to Magna Carta are included in Fourth of July orations, and in learned defenses of the Supreme Court. Yet

* Bentham, *Works* (Browning's Edition) I, p. 235; VI, p. 582; quoted in L. L. Fuller, "Legal Fictions," *Illinois Law Review,* XXV (1930), 363, 364.

who, that has ever read Magna Carta, whether in Latin or in English translation, has not been surprised at what he found there, and at how little he found there. And then when he studies the history and learns the background of the Charter, learns that it was annulled by the Pope a few months after it was sealed, and that King John who sealed it died a year after that event, he is puzzled further that the Charter has had such impact.

Scholars have debated whether the origin of trial by a jury of one's peers can be traced to the 39th article of Magna Carta. And it is far from clear what significance was attached to "the law of the land" in 1215 when those words were first written. We owe much to McIlwain and to McKechnie for light on these questions, and much further scholarship is being devoted to Magna Carta in this 750th anniversary year. But the fact remains that Magna Carta is not primarily significant for what it was, but rather for what it was made to be. It is the nature of man's habit of thought that when he seeks to bring about or to recognize change, he finds it easier if he can say with some measure of plausibility that what is new is simply an ancient truth. Magna Carta, at the very least, was the record of a successful struggle against royal power; and when new struggles against the King arose in seventeenth-century England, Magna Carta was a rock to tie to. Through Magna Carta it was possible for Coke to argue that what was new was in fact an old truth. Magna Carta became a symbol and a rallying point of great power. Magna Carta itself was unassailable, and thus what could be read into it took on much of the strength of the Charter itself. Thus Magna Carta became an important element in producing results which were never contemplated by barons or king at Runnymede.

A century later, influenced in part by Coke's writings, as well as by the history of the recent past, with which they were intimately familiar, our founding fathers, and their polemicists, made further use of Magna Carta, not for anything which it actually contained, but through what it had come to stand for, as the symbol of sanctioned limitation on royal power. The revolutionary colonists bolstered their consciences and their morale through invocation of Magna Carta, and in the process, one of its phrases—through translation into law French as *par due process de ley*—passed into our Constitution as the due process clause, which has so vitally affected not only judicial decisions in specific cases, but also our whole outlook on the proper function of government and the proper scope of governmental power.

Thus, though it may have been beyond the intention or the comprehension of any of those assembled at Runnymede in June 1215, and though it may be beyond its just deserts, Magna Carta has in fact been one of the great events in our legal and political history, and has a significance which has perhaps grown with each quarter-millennium. Its power is in no sense spent. It embodies an idea which we cherish, and its symbolic force moves on through the years.

Though Magna Carta is often taken for granted, and treated only as a symbol, it is important that it receive continuing thoughtful and critical examination, in order that its substance may be made clearer to us and its symbolical significance may be kept pure and unperverted. It was therefore fitting that the Annual Meeting of the American Council of Learned Societies in this anniversary year of 1965 should be devoted to a careful examination of the Charter and its significance by four leading scholars in the field. The addresses which they gave at this meeting form the contents of this book, and help to keep in focus this most typical and influential symbol of our political and governmental heritage. If we can remain true to Magna Carta and what it has come to signify over the past 750 years, we can look towards the next 750 years with confidence that the Charter will continue to serve us well as it has so powerfully and effectively in the past.

ERWIN N. GRISWOLD

Cambridge, Massachusetts
June 15, 1965

THE GREAT CHARTER

[1]

What Magna Carta Was

Samuel E. Thorne

𝕸agna Carta is a document of sixty-one independent clauses, strung together without much regard to orderly arrangement, revealing on its face no comprehensive or unifying design. It puts forward no single doctrine, says nothing of any constitutional plan or scheme of government. For a formula of politics, some theory of the state, we search it in vain. What we find instead—speaking generally, for its miscellaneous provisions cannot be summed up in a phrase—is a series of clauses regulating the relations between the king and the men of his realm. These latter are in general the tenants-in-chief, those who hold their great fiefs directly of the king, but the interests of others less exalted are not disregarded. The group which drew up the document was not composed solely of the great men of the realm.

The clauses themselves, each concerned with a distinct situa-

3

tion, limit the king's freedom of action severely. They forbid
some practices and restrict others, requiring things to be done or
not done, or done only in certain ways. They range very widely,
touching on many matters: the actions of royal officials, justices,
sheriffs, bailiffs, constables; the position of those who owe debts
to the Jews; the levying of scutages and tallages; recognitions of
novel disseisin and mort d'ancestor; amercements; disposition of
the property of those who die intestate, and of the lands of those
convicted of felony; establishment of proper measures for wine
and beer; destruction of fishweirs in the Thames; that the king is
not to sell, deny, or defer right or justice. A great many matters
are thus dealt with, all appearing cheek by jowl in one long and
disorderly jumble.

The document looks very much like answers given by many
persons to the questions "What is being done wrong" "What
practices should be halted?" "What improvements in administration should be adopted?—and that is indeed what it is. Magna
Carta does not represent the original baronial program; that is, it
was not for these provisions that the barons rebelled. The uprising had as its immediate cause the unwelcome prospect of a third
Norman campaign by John; more remote causes were long-
continued dissatisfaction with Angevin foreign policy and the in-
creasingly desperate state of Angevin fortunes. The purpose of
the revolt was to rid the country of John, a course not very different from the regicide that had been attempted three years before.
To depose John was not expected to be easy; on the other hand,
the king was far from anxious for a trial of strength, which
might, with French intervention, end disastrously for him. That
London had gone to the side of the rebels so easily and quickly
was an ominous sign.[1] The way was thus open to negotiation, and
through the intervention of Langton and a group of moderates
anxious to end the uprising, which had already begun, a compro-

4

mise was effected. The terms of the settlement appear in Magna
Carta, dated June 15, 1215, but no list of grievances, no concessions to be asked of the king, had been drawn up when the barons
renounced their homage on May 5, nor had any yet been formu-
lated when Langton and a few baronial representatives first met
with the king on May 31. Yet by June 10 the main points of the
agreement had been settled.[2] Thus it is likely that when the king
proved amenable to negotiation, which had not at first seemed
likely, many items were hurriedly assembled and thrown together. Though doubtless some of the clauses dealt with serious
grievances of long standing, which came readily to the minds of
all, others were of no great moment and cannot have weighed
heavily upon them.[3] Many of the men must have felt that the
document would not end the difficulties between themselves and
their king, others that no opportunity for a peaceful settlement
could be passed by. We cannot know if proposals were made
which the king rejected; it seems likely that at this lowest point in
his career he accepted whatever was asked. He may never have
expected to live up to them.

John was not only king of England and lord of Ireland, but
also, among other things, duke of Normandy, count of Anjou,
duke of Aquitaine, and count of Poitou—the lord of a domain
that stretched from the Scots border to the north of Spain.
Though we speak loosely of the Angevin empire, it was very far
from being a unified whole; Whatever unity this collection of fiefs
and lordships had was given it by the king. Before John came to
the throne, in 1199, the preservation of this heritage had become
the all-absorbing occupation of his brother Richard, who was
forced into holding and peace-keeping operations on a large scale.
A good number of the many battles the English were to have with
the ambitious and dangerous Philip Augustus, king of France,

had already been fought by the time of John's reign. English money in large amounts was already being poured into these continental dominions, supporting those loyal to the king, subsidizing those who might be brought to his side. By 1197 taxes in England had reached an all-time high, and almost all the expedients for raising money, for which John was ultimately to answer, were already in use.[4] Whether Englishmen were required to fight among strangers in far places was a troublesome question already pressing for solution. Did their feudal obligations require them and their men to fight in Aquitaine or Gascony? Many took the view that personal service extended only to the defense of the realm, or at most to service in the old Norman monarchy as it stood before the addition of the Angevin lands. Scutages—that is, money given in lieu of military service to support an army of mercenaries in the field—were easier to obtain.[5] The country groaned under these exactions, but the news that reached England was good: Richard's succession of victories, the recovery of Philip's conquests east of the Seine, the marvelous defeat of the French king at Gisors.

But where Richard had been invincible, John could do nothing right. No news of heroic action brightened the picture of recurrent defeats. The plain fact was that within five years of his accession he had lost his Norman inheritance. The story is straightforward; it is enough to say that he was engaged on two fronts, in Normandy and in Aquitaine, and that his position deteriorated rapidly. He seemed unable to prevent a long series of losses and his one great success at Mirabeau, the last English victory on French soil until the triumphs of Edward III, did little to postpone the end.

The reasons for Angevin failure in Normandy are difficult to assess. Norman sentiment was in favor of England. Many men owned land in both countries, and the two had long been bound together in a variety of ways. The country itself was well situated to withstand attack; its resources in men and money were considerable, and both could easily be reinforced across the Channel. In these circumstances, it should have been possible to save it, especially since the financial support John was able to call up was superior to that mustered by Philip Augustus. But on the English side there seems to have been some lack of leadership, an absence of commitment, which found no counterpart among the French.[6] Perhaps if the barons of Aquitaine and Gascony had been consistently loyal, if the counts of Flanders, Boulogne, and Toulouse had not deserted the Angevin alliance, an English victory would have been possible. These conditions, however, did not prevail; there were too many demands from too many places, too many weak points always needing to be shored up. Nor was anyone on the Continent anxious to take a firm stand against a powerful neighbor before an English victory was absolutely sure.

John returned to England in 1204 a defeated man, but one resolved to recoup his losses, firmly committed to a great plan for the recovery of Normandy, Touraine, and the old Angevin influence in the Midi. What he required more than anything else was money, and to accumulate the financial resources needed for this enterprise he was determined to turn everything to account. Though no military commander, John was an administrator of great skill and originality, especially in fiscal matters, and this talent was soon reflected in action. England began to feel an oppressiveness in government not hitherto experienced, certainly not on so large a scale. A new stringency was injected into the system; constantly re-examined for weak points and frequently reorganized to eliminate delays and loopholes, it recovered what was due the king rapidly and efficiently, with little possibility of escape. Even so, the accumulation proved inadequate, but for ten burdensome years every expedient was tried.[7]

The ordinary revenue of the Crown was derived from many sources; none of it depended on the consent of the baronage or on the consent of anyone else. Like any landowner, the king received the income from his property; like any landlord, he was entitled to the feudal incidents that attached to the lands his tenants held of him.[8] The relief, a payment an heir of full age was required to make in order to succeed to his father's fief, might be a very heavy charge. Wardships and marriages, the right to retain a minor heir's lands until he reached full age, and the right, as his guardian, to marry him or her off to the highest bidder, yielded substantial profits, especially if the matter was handled solely from the point of view of the fisc. The marriages of widows in the king's gift, particularly of those who owned substantial estates or held high places in aristocratic society, were a valuable source of income. The sum of 20,000 marks was proffered in 1214 by Geoffrey de Mandeville "for having Isabel countess of Gloucester to wife, with all the lands, tenements and fees belonging to the same Isabel." It was a high price, but she brought her husband an earldom and great wealth. Scutages yielded very substantial returns. The king had as well the right to tallage his demesne tenants at will, among them being the wealthy residents of boroughs (for example, the men of London), and in the same way to tallage the Jews, who were, so to speak, his chattels. The profits of justice were a fruitful source of revenue: payments could be taken not only to help a man recover what was his, but to save him from answering for what he possessed wrongfully. From the man who had earned the king's displeasure in some way, by some irregular action, real or imaginary, a sum fixed at the king's discretion might be legally exacted *pro benevolentia regis;* [9] and payment could be required of the man who sought a favor, an office in the king's gift, or any other advantage.

Many of these exactions, payments to the Crown, were not and could not be uniformly assessed. By their nature they varied from case to case, dependent upon particular circumstances, particular men, particular acts. Thus they lent themselves to other uses. A large relief might be exacted from one, a much smaller from another, though their holdings were roughly equivalent. The sum of 7,000 marks was demanded from John de Lacy for the succession to his father's lands in 1213, not because the king considered this a fair payment for the fiefs, but because De Lacy was suspect.[10] He was not, as John well knew, able to produce that sum and had to agree to the surrender of his castles as security until payment of the debt was complete. Furthermore, reliefs, wardships and marriages, and the other feudal incidents had not originated as tax measures. Their origin lay in the feudal law of property and their use to finance the conquest of Normandy, to support armies in Gascony, Aquitaine, and elsewhere, and to subsidize foreign allies had never been contemplated. The proper resource for such schemes lay in general taxation, in the feudal aid, like that granted for the defense of Normandy early in 1204. But such grants depended on baronial consent and good will and were no more likely to be forthcoming in the years before 1215 than they were for Henry III's Sicilian enterprise in 1258. John was thus forced to make do with these other sources of revenue, and to yield the sums he needed they had to be pushed to the limit.

John's tax policy with respect to the Jews will permit us to see his fiscal efforts in action.[11] Taxes had, of course, been levied on the Jews during the ten years of Richard's reign, but generally speaking, his demands were moderate. With the accession of John the picture changed considerably. He first exacted the high price of 4,000 marks for confirming their charters. In 1207 he took a tallage of 4,000 marks. In the same year he made a second demand, requiring Jewish moneylenders to pay a tenth of the value of their bonds. The basis of this second assessment was the

9

estimated value of debts due, each moneylender being required to furnish a list of his outstanding accounts and to pay a tenth of that total. Since liquid resources sufficient to pay that portion of total assets were seldom, if ever, available, the tallage required the calling in of loans on which the date of repayment had passed or on which no date had been fixed. The borrowers, who themselves lacked ready money, were thus compelled to raise it by the sale or lease of land, thereby putting the Jewish moneylender in funds, or alternatively, to make a composition or fine with the Crown, payments being credited to the Jewish lender's tax bill. The king was in fact taking the debts due the Jews into his own hands and collecting them directly. From John's point of view this represented an effort to get what he was entitled to: if the money had been where it ought to be, in the lender's pocket, he could have reached it; why should it not be taken directly?

The savage events of 1210 can only be accounted for on the supposition that the disclosures of their accounts by the moneylenders in 1207 were found to be, or imagined to be, inadequate or falsified. In 1210, Jews throughout England were suddenly imprisoned without warning of any kind, all males of any substance being lodged in jail. This action was accompanied by the seizure of their bonds, chirographs, and tallies, records of the debts they were owed. Later that year, after investigation had been made, a number of prominent Jews were found to have concealed or undervalued their accounts in 1207 and examples were made of them. Isaac of Norwich managed to purchase the king's favor by a fine of 10,000 marks, to be paid at a mark a day. He was stripped of all his possessions—his home, his bonds, and his chattels. Isaac of Canterbury was hanged. His chattels fetched no more than £30, and in 1223 the king disposed of his houses for 20 marks. There were others so dealt with. It is not surprising, therefore, that when John's new tallage, heavier than any yet levied in England, was placed on the Jews later in 1210, it yielded some 60,000 marks. All were required to contribute extravagantly, the sums being fixed by a royal agent's estimate of the taxpayer's total assets, an estimate not likely to err on the lenient side. The wealthier Jews, whose possessions had been seized, could only seek to mitigate the exactions to which they were subjected. The poorer, who had little to lose, seem in many cases to have fled the country. This was, of course, of little moment to the king, who was not anxious to retain those who were unprofitable to him.

The picture is clearly one of a king whose needs were great, who was avid for money and determined to exact the uttermost farthing. But it was not only the Jews who were heavily taxed in 1210, for in that year John took a scutage with respect to his Irish campaign that yielded 10,000 marks and a tallage on cities, towns, and the royal demesne that yielded 12,000. There is, indeed, no reason to believe that Jews were, on the whole, more liable to arbitrary exactions than Christians. Though the harsh exactions described might seem to indicate the unreasonable oppression of an unpopular community which lay at the mercy of its royal protector, the king in fact dealt in a ruthless manner with Christians and Jews alike, discriminating between them in no way. All paid, or were forced to undertake to pay, enormous sums.

It is evident that the necessities of King John drove him to severities that had been unknown in the preceding century. The Jews had been taxed before but never, so far as the records indicate, pressed to realize their assets. Nor had borrowers earlier been forced to repay secured loans their bankers had been satisfied to carry. Furthermore, John did not scruple to collect the interest on Jewish loans when they came into his hand, though the taking of interest was forbidden to Christians and roundly condemned by the Church. (By Magna Carta, chapter 10 he was limited to recovering only the principle on loans. By chapter 11 he was required to allow a widow whose husband who had been indebted to the Jews, and whose debt the king was now collecting, to have her dower before the debt was completely paid; that is, he was required to exclude the income from her dower from that available for the reduction of the debt, and also to provide necessities for the children of the deceased while the land was in his hand. These concessions had apparently not been customary before.)

On August 16, 1212, John learned of the baronial plot against his life. His opponents planned to murder him in Wales, either directly or by deserting him in the face of the enemy.[12] This was no spur-of-the-moment attempt, but a carefully planned and organized action for which there was extensive support. When it failed, since the plan had required no elaborate preparatory steps susceptible of proof, most of the conspirators escaped detection. The complicity of a handful was clear, but the king had his suspicions about others, and, in the light of later events, they proved in the main well founded. Within a week Richard de Umfraville had surrendered his castle at Prudhoe and his four sons as hostages for his faithful service. On the day following, Earl David of Huntingdon surrendered his castle at Fotheringhay, and before a month had passed a dozen men had put their castles and their sons or daughters in the king's hand.

There can be no doubt that John was shaken by the seriousness of the situation. The chroniclers indicate that he promised many things—to remit the new forest exactions, to limit the exactions of his foresters to those customary in the reign of his father, not to force widows to marry against their will (or, at any rate, to treat them less rigorously), to limit the exactions of his sheriffs, to deal more favorably with those who owed debts to the Jews.[13]

But not much seems to have come of these promises. Certainly by November John was again busy with plans for the large-scale expedition scheduled for the spring, and was forming new alliances with the princes of the Low Countries. Despite widespread baronial opposition to his continental plans, openly and generally expressed, he proceeded implacably toward perfecting them. He doubtless expected to deal with the opposition in the usual way, person by person as the occasion warranted, by harshness or concession, by the restoration of inheritances on hard terms or on easy, by the release of hostages, grants of wardships, acquittances of debts, and the rest of the weapons in his armory. Again he was successful, though for other reasons his continental expedition had to be postponed.

On February 9 or 10, 1214, he sailed for Poitou to participate in the recovery of his lost dominions. By the end of July all was lost, for by then his continental alliance, into which he had put such effort and sunk so much money, had collapsed on the battlefield of Bouvines. Thus, ten years after the loss of Normandy, John's scheme to recover it through a grand European coalition against France was shipwrecked, seriously loosening his hold on his other continental domains as well. "Bouvines helped England become a constitutional country," Trevelyan writes,[14] "and helped reduce the possessions of the English kings abroad to reasonable size. The consequent return to a more insular outlook saved it from too close an identification with France, and kept the energies and thoughts of its leaders from being drawn away from national interests and internal problems." That is true, but it was hardly the view England then took of the situation. John had been defeated in the objective toward which, during the ten furious years between 1204 and 1214, the whole of his administrative and diplomatic effort had been directed. The unavoidable product of that effort had been ever-increasing unrest and dissatisfaction among the English baronage, provoked by the manifold ways in which John had exploited their resources to support Angevin policy and possessions abroad. It was now seen that the expedients, the stringencies, the oppressions, had been suffered for nothing; that the burdens, once thought temporary, to be borne only until the certain victory they guaranteed had been achieved, were not to be remitted in the foreseeable future.

This John confirmed on his return to England in October 1214: the war must be resumed, new treasure built up, new allies sought, new expeditions planned. How he could have said anything else and not opened the way to the loss of the remainder of his continental dominions it is difficult to see. But if his words, intended for his allies abroad, were greeted with enthusiasm there, they were received with dismay in England. A third attempt, on a larger scale, to regain and retain Normandy was not to be countenanced. Events now began to move with great rapidity. Rebellion was not far off, and during the winter of 1214 and the early months of 1215 John, sensitive to the change, made military preparations for meeting it.[15] At the same time he pursued a policy of making concessions, gifts, and loans where they would be of value; of granting pardons for debts, licenses, wardships, and marriages to those he considered good political investments. Since his abilities as a politician and administrator were great, he faced the difficulties with energy and skill. He had many favors to bestow and much patronage to dispense. Nor did the great lords who were against him come into the open at once. It was dangerous business. But when a group of leading men formally renounced their homage to the king in May 1215, and London came over to them within a fortnight, the landslide could no longer be halted. When the rebels came face to face with John at Runnymede on June 15, there were many among them whose open support of the baronial cause was only a few months old; in some cases its duration could be computed in weeks, even days. This large-scale defection to the rebel cause following the capitulation of London compelled the king to negotiate.

It is, of course, false to speak of the charter forced on a king deserted by the nation, alone except for a handful of mercenary captains. No head of state, even under the most despotic kind of personal government, has ever been completely bereft of friends and supporters. The counselors whose names are set out in the preamble of Magna Carta, who had for years been conspicuous in the government of King John, were unquestionably on the side of the Crown. It is likewise a mistake to think that the baronial opposition as a whole believed that with the king's seal set to the draft agreement the object of their revolt had been achieved. Not Magna Carta, but the abandonment of John's continental designs or his removal, had been the baronial program; that is why, after the document had been secured, there was no general rejoicing and many remained suspicious and hostile.[16] King John was equally so; having conceded much, he was incensed to find that his concessions had failed to produce the unity of purpose, the wholehearted backing of his plans, that Langton and the others had encouraged him to anticipate. To many of the barons, the charter, the compromise to which they had come, seemed inadequate. Disillusioned with the Angevin regime, what they wanted was to rid themselves of King John. They were already in touch with Philip of France, whose son they hoped to make their new king, thus ending all possibility of continued conflict in France forever. This was an improvement over the regicide to which they had pinned their hopes three years before, but as an extreme course it had not won over a majority of the barons. Even to the majority, however, it was clear that the clauses of the charter did not touch the real issue between themselves and their king: distrust and lack of confidence. It was a makeshift. No document, no list of concessions, however long, was likely to make John into a good lord to his people. In this they were correct. By birth and position he was committed to a policy that precluded him from giving his energy and thought, his kind and benign consideration, solely to English interests. But still the barons, by answering the questions "What are your objections to John, not generally, but specifically?" "What concessions would satisfy you?" "With what safeguards would you be content to have him remain on the throne?" had unwittingly taken their first step away from the past, the vague and unworkable concept of "good lordship," and turned their faces toward the future, a king limited by concessions made to the governed, a king bound by specific restrictions, a king under law.

Not quite a month after the signing of Magna Carta, John asked the Pope to quash the concessions forced upon him. They had not seemed exorbitant when deposition was in the air, but they were now impossible to bear. On August 24, a little more than two months after the reconciliation at Runnymede, Innocent III declared the charter not only a "shameful and demeaning agreement, forced upon the king by violence and fear," but "illegal and unjust." "Therefore," he went on to say, "we utterly reject and condemn this settlement, and under threat of excommunication order that the king not dare to observe it nor the barons require it to be observed. The charter, we hereby declare to be a nullity, void of all validity forever." [17]

The tangled story of the last twelve months of John's life has often been told and I need not repeat it here. With the disappearance of the charter, the civil war it had temporarily averted began again in earnest. Louis of France was proclaimed king and his invasion force, with baronial help, swept all before it. On October 18 John died, leaving the country in turmoil and a boy of nine as his successor. On November 12 the charter was reissued by the young king's advisers, thus cutting the ground from beneath the feet of Louis. It was perhaps only a piece of expediency, but the haphazard statement of rights and regulations, the miscellaneous collection of practical remedies, now began a long career. It was to be a magnificent one.

It is often said that the charter contained no radical proposals but was simply a return to ancient custom. But many radical proposals come disguised as returns to the past,[18] and few would say that a proposal limiting the government of this country to the taxes and rates of 1905 was not radical. The innovations in our tax structure since that date have been legally made, but so were the innovations made by the Angevin kings. Though burdensome in the extreme, they had been introduced after due deliberation to support what the government considered legitimate and necessary ends. Not all Englishmen agreed on those ends, but whether England went to war, supported armies abroad, subsidized foreign allies, was not a matter for them but for the king and his advisers. More than that, he paid the bill out of his own pocket, out of funds which were his due and which his subjects could not lawfully withhold from him. If he was obdurate, rebellion was the only course open, rebellion and the substitution of a new king who would be a good lord to his people. That the old could be limited by a document, that his power could be circumscribed and restricted, was a plan that had not yet been tried, that held great promise for the future. Did the magnates see that? Did they see that by reduction of the king's independent income he could be made dependent on them? John perhaps saw something of the sort, for he said the charter took the crown of England from him. That is untrue, but it is proper to say that, unwittingly and at first unsuccessfully, a great step toward accomplishing that end had been taken.

NOTES

1 May 17, 1215. The barons had renounced their homage on May 5, at which time the war had begun.

2 James C. Holt, "The Making of Magna Carta," *English Historical Review,* LXXII (1957), 401.

3 James C. Holt, *The Northerners: A Study in the Reign of King John* (Oxford, 1961), p. 111; G. O. Sayles and H. G. Richardson, *The Governance of Mediaeval England* (Edinburgh, 1963), p. 389.

4 Holt, *The Northerners,* pp. 146 ff.

5 *Ibid.,* pp. 88, 91.

6 F. M. Powicke, *The Loss of Normandy* (Manchester, 1961), p. 249.

7 Holt, *The Northerners,* pp. 72, 163 ff; B. E. Harris, "King John and the Sheriffs' Farms," *English Historical Review,* LXXIX (1964), 532.

8 For what follows see A. L. Poole, *Obligations of Society in the Twelfth and Thirteenth Centuries* (Oxford, 1946), p. 97.

9 Holt, *The Northerners,* p. 177.

10 *Ibid.*

11 H. G. Richardson, *The English Jewry under Angevin Kings* (London, 1960), pp. 166 ff.

12 Holt, *The Northerners,* pp. 83 ff.

13 *Ibid.*

14 G. M. Trevelyan, *History of England* (London, 1926), p. 168.

15 Holt, *The Northerners,* pp. 104-7, 110.

16 *Ibid.,* pp. 120 ff.

17 Christopher R. Cheney and W. H. Semple, eds., *Selected Letters of Pope Innocent III* (London, 1953), p. 216.

18 James C. Holt, "The Barons and the Great Charter," *English Historical Review,* LXX (1955), 18-19.

[II]

Magna Carta & British Constitutionalism

William H. Dunham, Jr.

The part that Magna Carta played after 1300 in the progression of British constitutionalism was minor, but it was by no means insignificant. First of all, the Great Charter was a living idea and a lively one, and it helped to build up two cardinal constitutional principles—government by agreement, or contract, and the rule of law. Then the "form and tenor" of Magna Carta, for over three centuries, 1300-1600, provided an undefined and all-embracing authority that took the place of a constitution. As such, it afforded to some degree the certainty in law and the consistency in governance that seventeenth-century jurists hoped to find in what they called "the fundamental law," and what they succeeded in finding, after the Glorious Revolution of 1689, in the British Constitution.

The word "constitution," meaning a frame or form of government, first appeared, but only intermittently, in the seventeenth century. Not until the 1680s did the term begin to convey the idea of a set of fundamental principles according to which men govern a state or nation. After 1689, Britons attributed their modern constitution to the Glorious Revolution. In 1812, Horace Twiss wrote of "the revolution in 1688, when this constitution [of 1812] was originally established."[1] Even earlier, Englishmen had claimed, and believed, that their constitution and their government were "founded upon the Revolution," and in the eighteenth century "the Revolution Settlement" supplanted "the form and tenor of Magna Carta" as a sanction of constitutional government. The British were convinced that they had a constitution, not only because they wished to have one, but because visiting continentals, like Montesquieu, Voltaire, and De Lolme, had become ecstatic over its imagined virtues. To ascertain whether the British then had, or even now have, a constitution is difficult. Nonetheless, many Englishmen today think that they have one—after all, Dicey, Holdsworth, and Jennings have told them so. In any event, all of them certainly believe in the cult of constitutionalism—a word first used to mean "a constitutional system of government" in 1832, and one that came to denote in 1871, "adherence to constitutional principles."[2]

The genesis of modern constitutionalism goes back before Magna Carta, and King John's Charter of 1215 only marks a point of recognition in the formulation of several such principles. King Alfred in the ninth century wrote about and, of course, believed in the supremacy of law; and he expected his judges to follow established procedures. These two principles men were later to designate as the supremacy of statute and the due process of the law; and during the reign of Elizabeth I they were conjoined to form the concept of the rule of law.[3] Elements of a contract, the king's coronation oath and the subject's oath of fidelity or allegiance, appeared in the tenth century. Eventually, these two unilateral obligations combined in men's minds to create the idea of a bilateral agreement. This mutual engagement was, perhaps, "the original contract" that the revolutionaries of 1689 alleged King James II to have broken; and it certainly was the "implied contract" upon which Blackstone, in 1765, based his definition of allegiance.

This contractual principle, with its corollaries counsel and consent, for long has been the cornerstone of government by agreement. However, only the collateral principles of majority rule and of representation have made this kind of government feasible. Chapter 61 of King John's Magna Carta explicitly recognized majority decisions, decisions by the greater number of the twenty-five barons appointed to enforce the Charter against an erring king. This chapter provided that whatsoever the greater part of the committee agreed upon, that was to be held established just as if all twenty-five had consented thereto. Along with this express recognition of majority rule went an implied acknowledgment of its corollaries—criticism, opposition, and dissent. These are the very virtues of constitutionalism upon which the individual's freedom in the twentieth century so delicately depends. Moreover, the same chapter 61 provided a procedure for distraining a king and his officers who had done wrong, in order to procure redress for the subject. Here, in an attempt to make the king and his government accountable for wrongs already done, the authors of the Great Charter took for granted the proposition that the king, as ruler, was responsible for righting wrongs and doing justice.

The principle of responsibility, and ultimately of responsible government itself, had as their foundation a belief in government by agreement, by contract. The contractual principle doubtless owed something to the feudal contract between the king and his tenants-in-chief; and yet the constitutional concept of a contract, a covenant, or an engagement, a Roman *sponsio*, it seems, owed much more to the bond between the king and his subjects. The subject's oath of fidelity, of allegiance, bound him as a subject to the king; and the king's coronation oath to confirm his promise to hold, to keep, and to strengthen the laws obligated him to God and, perhaps, to that medieval abstraction "the people." Moreover, a sequence of coronation charters from Henry I's on through Stephen's and Henry II's looked like and sounded in contract. Then Henry III's advisers perpetuated the idea of agreement in their first reissue of Magna Carta in November 1216, a fortnight after they had crowned the nine-year-old king. At a king's coronation, the earls and barons, and later on the peers of the realm, did their homage and swore fidelity to the king as both feudal lord and royal sovereign. The audience, for the people, shouted *Vivat rex, vivat rex,* and agreed explicitly that the king should be crowned; implicitly and tacitly, they accepted his rule and reign.

Eventually, the two elements of contract, these two unilateral obligations, the subject's promise to the king and the king's to God, combined in men's minds to form a bilateral agreement. Blackstone, in his *Commentaries on the Laws of England,* called it "an implied contract with the prince, that so long as the one [the king] affords protection, so long the other [the subject] will demean himself faithfully." [4] More recently, Queen Elizabeth II, in her 1953 Christmas Message to her subjects throughout all her lands, described the Crown as "not merely an abstract symbol of our unity but a personal and living bond between you and me." [5] This personal connection between the sovereign and the subject created in theory a doctrine of mutual obligation and in practice what Powicke so sagaciously styled "the joint-enterprise of government."

In this contractual principle, Magna Carta's role was not exclusive, and yet it was of consequence. The fact of Magna Carta, more than the particulars of its contents, and the forty-four or more confirmations before 1416 were what lent strength and support to the contractual idea. Each of the early confirmations of the Great Charter, like Edward I's in 1297 in exchange for a money grant and again in 1301 when the magnates "were powerful enough to draw out the contractual understanding implied by taxation," as Powicke put it, was the product of bargaining. At the 1301 Lincoln parliament, Edward I agreed to observe the charters and to annul and void any statutes to the contrary. Then, "on condition that the aforesaid matters are carried out . . . the people of the realm grant him a fifteenth in place of the twentieth recently granted." Such recapitulations and rehearsals of the subject's rights and liberties, and of the mutual obligations with the king, in both their generality and their particularity, made a truly formal engagement. Chapter 60 of King John's Charter recognized this mutuality in requiring that the king's observance of liberties and customs towards his men "shall be observed by all of our kingdom, as well clergy as laymen, as far as pertains to them, towards their men." The conditional nature of the 1215 agreement between the two parties, *ex parte regis* and *ex parte baronum,* acquired an even greater specificity in the final version of 1225. At that time Henry III's advisers added to this chapter the words: "Moreover, for this grant and gift of these liberties . . . the archbishops, bishops, abbots, priors, earls, barons, knights, free tenants, and all [men] of our realm have given us [the king] a fifteenth part of all their moveables." Henry III struck a similar bargain in January 1237 when he promised, as the express condition for the grant of a thirtieth, that the "liberties of Magna Carta" should be observed inviolably.[6]

Confirmation was to follow confirmation, and although men forgot the Charter's specific contents, they recalled its purport, and this they designated its "tenor and form." Thus the series of over forty confirmations came to create a historical continuum, and this in fact constituted a contract. The first chapter of the first statute of Richard II's first parliament, in 1377, begins: "First, it is agreed and established . . . that the Great Charter which at the request of the said commons was read in the said parliament . . . and all other good ordinances and statutes . . . be held and firmly kept." Subsequently, enrollments on the Statute Roll became simpler as repetition, if not ennui, eroded away word after word. In 1416 the clerk entered as an enacted statute the brief formula, "that the Great Charter and the Charter of the Forest, and all other good statutes and ordinances . . . not repealed shall be firmly held and kept in all points." What the confirmation of the charters had come to mean was, in short, that the king and his government accepted as an obligation the stipulation that the law—certainly the statutes—should rule over all. Moreover, several fourteenth-century acts of Parliament sought to clarify the meaning of the phrase "process of law," and before the century ended men had expanded these three words into the eternal slogan "the due process of the law."

The recognition of Magna Carta as a statute made it an operative force in building up the doctrine of due process and then in converting that principle into the grander formula, the rule of law. Edward I in his confirmation of 1297 had agreed that the king's courts should admit "the Great Charter of Liberties as common law," and that any judgment contrary to the Charter be held for nought.[7] Thenceforth, justices, pleaders, and parliament-men applied various chapters of the Charter as statute law, and

they cited Henry III's 1225 version, greatly shortened from 63 to
37 chapters, as the statute, "9 Henry III." By making Magna
Carta into a statute, men preserved it as an idea whose potency
increased as both bench and bar cited, interpreted, misinterpreted,
and extended its original meaning. In this way, through the
courts, the Great Charter became associated with the great principles of modern constitutionalism—contract and the rule of law
—and augmented their force, virtue, and effect. Chapter 39, for
example, contained the famed phrase "by the lawful judgement of
his peers and/or by the law of the land." For over four hundred
years jurists and scholars glossed this clause, and they gave it an
exegesis of its own. By so doing, their expositions served to clarify
and to define, and above all to enrich the meaning of the concept,
lawful procedure. They put broad constructions upon the phrases
"judgement of peers" and "the law of the land," and they made
them synonymous with the course of the law and the process of
law.

First, the phrase "by the lawful judgement of his peers," that is,
his equals, required for its fulfillment a judicial process, one already recognized as lawful. Then the words "by the law of the
land" intended that prosecutions or actions the king and his ministers might take against any freeman must be through procedures duly recognized as according to the law. Even a king was
not to interfere with the course of the law or lawful procedures,
and the reforming Ordinances of 1311 (chapter 28) contained,
perhaps for the first time in a constitutional context, the words, in
French, *process de ley*.[8] Through the fourteenth century men
confused the two key phrases of chapter 39. Once they combined
them into "by process of his peers." [9] In the 1350s parliaments
passed statutes to define chapter 39, and an act of 1352 explained
what the phrase "by the law of the land" meant, to wit: "by indictment of good and lawful people . . . in due manner, or by

process made by original writ at the common law; . . . [or] by the course of the law." [10] Later, in 1378, the commons complained that a certain ordinance was "openly against the Great Charter . . . [and the provision] that no freeman can be taken or imprisoned without due process of law." [11] These broad constructions and generous interpretations had become widespread by 1415. In that year the good people of Sandwich invoked Magna Carta against the constable of Dover and recited that no man might be judged "except by the common law" and that he should not be "molested or injured without due process of law." [12]

Richard II's deposition in 1399 had highlighted the danger— no matter whether real or imagined—to which he had exposed the doctrine of due process. Arbitrary government at the king's arbitrary discretion had jeopardized the security of the principles that Magna Carta was advancing—contract and the rule of law. The thirty-three articles that the Lancastrians drew up to justify their deposition of Richard II reflect Magna Carta's accomplishment.[13] Only one article names the Charter specifically, that referring to the "liberties of the Church approved in Magna Carta"; but several others mention the kingdom's "liberties," and even more assume the principles implicit in the Great Charter. The Lancastrian apologia alleged that King Richard had broken such principles-in-the-making as: the consent of the estates of the realm, the king's promise or contract sworn in his coronation oath, governance *per legem terrae,* and lawful process (*processu legitimo*). Perhaps the reason why Magna Carta did not loom larger in Richard II's deposition is that its task of supporting and augmenting the principles of government by agreement and of the rule of law had been done, and done effectively. The Lancastrians treated as breach of contract Richard's failure to repay money borrowed from his subjects, and his enemies recorded that he "had not fulfilled his promise." Breaking his coronation oath

and dilapidating the crown's rights, goods and possessions vio-
lated the king's obligations. The theme that runs through these
accusations was that the king had stepped outside the law and
above it. He had in specific instances, such as the executions of
the duke of Gloucester and the earls of Arundel and Warwick,
punished men "without answer or lawful process whatsoever."

The principle of due process drew strength and vigor from
Magna Carta, especially from chapter 39, which men cited as a
statute. Yet paradoxically, the making of Magna Carta into a statute may explain its apparent eclipse in the fifteenth century and
its revival in the sixteenth. Men cited this statute, by antiquity the
greatest of them all, in court along with others, and such constant
usage reduced it to almost, but never quite, a parity with its fel-
lows. Pleaders who cited articles of the Charter before the king's
justices as part of the common law made it their property; and
Readers at the Inns of Court kept new generations of barristers
aware of the Charter's existence and so assured its survival. Sir
Robert Brook, early in Queen Mary's reign, gave two Readings
on chapters 38 and 24, and another Reader, probably Sir Thomas
Williams, the Lent Reader at the Inner Temple in 1557-58, introduced "the Statute of Magna Carta which I mean by your pa-
tience and favours to read upon." Williams, thrice a member of
Parliament, added history to his legal teaching and told his listen-
ers why King John had granted the Great Charter. "There were
almost none of the said ancient laws of this realm put in use," he
explained, and so the nobles and subjects "did think that the king
had thereby not only encroached upon the liberties of the Church,
but also had otherwise done many wrongs and injuries unto
divers of his subjects, contrary to the said ancient laws of this
realm." [14]

Readers at the Inns of Court during James I's reign continued
to put Magna Carta's sanction upon the rule of law. Francis Ash-

ley, the Autumn Reader at the Middle Temple in 1616, gave a most elaborate lecture in eight divisions upon the liberty of the subject, notably on Magna Carta's chapter 39. He eulogized this "law of laws" and declared that "if it be a mere statute, it is the statute of statutes, for it hath begotten many of the like kind." In several places, Ashley's Reading reached a high pitch of eloquence, one that sustained the common lawyers' claims for the Great Charter against both civilians and ecclesiastics: "If we love our liberty," Ashley declared, "no one shall be taken or imprisoned. . . . If we would enjoy the benefit of the laws in general, no one shall be outlawed; or if we rejoice in the air of our own country, no one shall be exiled . . . except by lawful judgement of equals and/or the law of the land." To protect life itself "against the mischiefs of power and art," Ashley quoted the famous words of chapter 39, and then concluded, "in brief, by virtue of this statute we have property in our goods, title to our lands, liberty for our persons, and safety for our lives." Then the learned Lecturer laid down for the young men of law before him his moral: "no man shall be punished before he be condemned; and no man shall be condemned before he be heard; and none shall be heard but his just defense allowed." [15] Here was what the rule of law in its narrower, professional sense had come to mean by 1616.

However, the rule of law alone, even in the hands of lawyers, was not enough to preserve the subjects' liberties nor to assure Englishmen that there would be any British constitutionalism. What had happened was that these men of law, by making Magna Carta into a statute, had confined it to the Inns of Court and the courts of common law. There the Great Charter slumbered—I will not say "bed-rid" as Sir Benjamin Rudyerd did in 1628 when he became exceeding glad "to see it walk abroad

again with new vigour and luster."[16] However, a political
awakening had occurred back in Henry VIII's reign, and men had
brought Magna Carta out into the light of politics and parliament. *The Great Charter of the Freedoms of the Realm,* to use
the English title in a parliamentary petition of 1429, compre-
hended the underlying assumptions—so well understood, yet so
ill-defined—and the broad principles of governance that made up
its form and tenor.[17] Men made of these catchwords a shibboleth,
a political slogan, and an undefined goal. In their desire for certainty in public law, they gave to Magna Carta an inviolability of
its own; and in their quest for consistency in the rules of governance, they made of the Great Charter a criterion by which to
determine right law from wrong, and the unjust from the fair.

The form and tenor of Magna Carta offered a cover of authority for the rules and principles of Tudor government that were in
fact, though not in name, a constitution. In Henry VIII's time,
Stephen Gardiner, bishop of Winchester, advised the king not to
change "the form of his reign" [rule], for "by this form of government you be established . . . and it is agreeable with the nature of your people." Then the bishop added, "if you begin a new
manner of policy, how it will frame, no man can tell; and how
this [one] frameth you can tell; and [I] would never advise your
grace to leave a certain for an uncertain." To sanction such cer-
tainties, Tudor lawyers and statesmen turned again to Magna
Carta. Here they found a taboo which forbade things repugnant
to its form and tenor, and they made of it a substitute for a constitution. One of the charges brought against Cardinal Wolsey, at
the time of his fall in 1529, "was, that he had granted injunctions
to stay the common laws." Bishop Gardiner recorded further,
"upon that occasion Magna Carta was spoken of, and it was made
a great matter the stay of the common law."[18] A few years later,

at his trial in 1535, Sir Thomas More set the Charter up as a test of the validity of the statute upon which the Crown had grounded his indictment. More claimed this act of Parliament to be "directly repugnant to the laws of God and his holy church" and "contrary both to the laws and statutes of our own land yet unrepealled, as they might evidently perceive in Magna Charta." Here Sir Thomas, a former Speaker of the House of Commons and an ex-chancellor, conservatively took his stand upon Edward III's statute of 1368 which had declared, "if any statute be made to the contrary [of Magna Carta], that shall be holden for none." Two centuries after Sir Thomas' death, John Adams in 1765 took the same stand in the Braintree instructions and declared that the Stamp Act was "directly repugnant to the Great Charter itself." [19]

The connection between Magna Carta and Parliament was in part a product of the myths that lawyers, historians, and chroniclers had created. Caxton's *Chronicles,* first printed in 1480, placed Henry III's "confirmation of King John's charter" at "a great parliament." Furthermore, Caxton stressed the contractual nature of the bargain: "for the grant of these two charters, prelates, earls and barons, and all the commons of England gave to the king a thousand marks of silver." [20] A century later, in 1577, Holinshed located Henry III's granting of the 1225 charter and his subsequent confirmations at parliaments. [21] The pens of learned Elizabethans, like William Lambarde, continued to augment the antiquity of Parliament and to increase its stature. This treatiser claimed that Parliament in 1225 had included "the king, peers, and commons of this land" when Henry III had granted "The Great Charter of England . . . for which the English men had no less striven, than the Trojans for their Helena." More significant, perhaps, Lambarde went on to prove that the Charter "was made by the common consent of all the realm." [22] Thus bad history had begun to make good law by exalting the Great Charter into a still grander contract and by putting statute law and Parliament into the ascendant.

This Elizabethan revival of Magna Carta had begun in the 1580s, and for over fifty years the Charter enjoyed an Indian summer. Common lawyers, especially those with Puritan clients, and the civil lawyers who practiced in chancery and in the church courts, and their episcopal sponsors wrangled over its chapters and their meaning. The Puritans, during the 1570s, had taken their cause into the political arena of Parliament, and soon they included Magna Carta in many of the bills they introduced. One such bill was intended to prevent anyone from being imprisoned or "put to answer, but only by due course of the laws, statutes, and ancient laudable customs of the realm and not otherwise." The queen's progenitors had "granted and confirmed" these laws and liberties, this bill explained, "by the Great Charter commonly called Magna Carta." [23] The Puritans sought to make Magna Carta fundamental and unalterable. Robert Beale, clerk of the privy council, member of Parliament, and a civil lawyer, held "the law of laws" to be "Magna Carta against which I trust neither any common or ecclesiastical lawyer will make any exception at all." With Sir James Morice, another member of Parliament, Beale cited Edward III's statute that no man shall be attached "contrary to the form of the Great Charter"; and Beale (sounding very modern) went on to "infer that by the statute of Magna Charta and the old laws of this realm, this oath for a man to accuse himself was and is utterly inhibited." [24] Soon after, in 1589, Morice presented a bill in Parliament entitled, "For confirmation of a branch of Magna Charta." "Her Majesty's subjects, without any suit or lawful process or arrest, or without . . . ordinary and due course and proceeding in law," the preamble declared, "have been committed to prison . . . contrary to the

Great Charter and ancient good laws and statutes of this Realm." [25]

To refute these Puritans, in parliaments and courts, Crown lawyers and ecclesiastics also turned to the authority and prestige of Magna Carta. Once Archbishop Whitgift (Elizabeth "called him her little black husband") appropriated chapter 1 guaranteeing the liberties of the English Church and then turned the Charter back against the queen herself. To check those courtiers who were seeking out concealed Church lands which they might acquire through forfeiture to the Crown, Whitgift, while still bishop of Worcester, referred the queen to Magna Carta. There she would find, so the bishop told her, that she, like her predecessors, had been sworn at her coronation "to maintain the church's lands, and the rights belonging to it; and this testified openly at the holy altar by laying her hand upon the Bible, there lying before her. And that many modern statutes denounced a curse [an excommunication] against those that break Magna Charta." Then this zealous defender of the Church and its property added, "and what account could be given for that breach of the oath at the great day either by her majesty or himself . . . he knew not." [26] At the end of the century, about 1598, bishops and others exercising ecclesiastical jurisdiction drew up several propositions. One of them questioned whether the "liberties and franchises of the church . . . by virtue of these statutes and Magna Charta ought not still to be holden as inviolable as ever they were." [27]

The dean of Whitgift's own court of arches, Dr. Richard Cosin, a civil lawyer, also cited Magna Carta with freedom, indeed, abandon. He might appeal to chapter 1 to defend the Church's rights and liberties; then again, he had little difficulty in finessing chapter 39 by simply declaring, with somewhat arrogant assurance, "it is manifest, that the words have no relation to the jurisdiction ecclesiastical." [28] Against Beale's claim for the Charter's inviolability and supremacy, the dean set forth the proposition that the law of Magna Carta was not immutable. Here Cosin, a civilian, anticipated Blackstone's doctrine of the sovereignty of statute and of the statute-making body, Parliament. "Albeit Magna Carta had been to the contrary," Dr. Cosin contended in his tract, "yet an act of parliament coming after, might change that law"; and he further added, "none authority can so bind itself by any law; but that (upon good occasion and by like power) it may be abrogated again." [29]

Crown lawyers, too, had resorted to Magna Carta as ultimate authority. Sir Francis Bacon with Attorney-General Hobart in 1613 used the Great Charter to sanction the royal prerogative. Just as the ecclesiastics let the law of the land embrace the laws of the Church, as Henry VIII's statutes logically required, so did the king's counsel let the *lex terre* comprehend the *lex coronae.* In 1613, Bacon and Hobart opened a case by denying that chapter 39 limited royal actions against the subjects' bodies, goods, or lands to legal proceedings in the ordinary courts of justice. They stated that this proposition was "not only grossly erroneous and contrary to the rules of law, but dangerous and tending to the dissolving of government." Then they interpreted the law of the land of chapter 39 to include the regal power: "his majesty's prerogative and his absolute power incident to his sovereignty is also *lex terrae,* and is invested and exercised by the law of the land, and is part thereof." [30] Thus the Stuart king's men of law decided to appropriate, rather than to repudiate, both the rule of law and Magna Carta. Lord Chancellor Ellesmere, in 1615, interpreted the phrase "the law of the land" to include what he called "matters of conscience and equity which cannot be remedied by the strict rules of the common law." [31] When lawyers, both for the Crown and for its opponents, parliament-men, and Church of England clergy all found authority in Magna Carta for their divergent views, then surely the Great Charter's virtue was becoming compromised.

Instead of Magna Carta's saving constitutionalism, constitutionalism, it would seem, was working through Parliament and the courts to preserve the Great Charter's force, virtue, and effect. A bill in 1606 headed, "An Act for the due Observance of the Great Charter," is in itself evidence that the Charter's authority was waning. The bill intended "that if any judgement should be given contrary to the tenor of the said Great Charter, that the same should be undone and holden for nought." [32] Already, in 1601, Sir Edward Coke, still a young man on the make, had invoked Magna Carta to sanction lawful procedure in a eulogy of both the Charter and the queen. "[She] governeth her people by God's goodness, in peace and prosperity by these laws, and punisheth not the greatest offender . . . but by the just and equal proceedings of law . . . bless God, for Queen Elizabeth, whose continual charge . . . is, that for no commandment under the great or privy seal, writs or letters, common right be disturbed or delayed . . . and this agreeth with the ancient law of England, declared by the Great Charter." [33] Such grandiloquence might team up the sacred queen and the holy Charter; but when all sides, between 1590 and 1630, found in its form and tenor the legality they were looking for, then a dissipation of Magna Carta's full force and effect had begun.

Moreover, by that time the Great Charter was by no means the only authority men called upon to justify their aspirations. When the Puritans in 1606 presented to Parliament the bill for the observance of Magna Carta, they sought to void twenty-three of the canons that the Church of England had adopted in 1604. These new rules, they claimed, were "hurtful to the prerogative royal, onerous to the people, contrarient to the said Great Charter and other laws, statutes, liberties, and free customs of this realm." [34] In the next year, 1607, Nicholas Fuller acted as counsel for Puritan clients in several test cases. In one, he contended that this "Charter, by divers other statutes after, is confirmed, with such strong enforcements in some of them, as to make void such statutes, as should be contrary to Magna Charta." [35] Nevertheless, Fuller lost his case, and the judges ruled that imprisonment by the court of high commission was lawful. Two years later Attorney-General Hobart cited the judgment in Fuller's case and contended that it had overruled Magna Carta. He concluded that to allege chapter 39 to be against imprisonment by the high commission "is out of season, because this latter law [the decision against Fuller] abrogates the former and the statutes are infinite that have given imprisonment in sundry cases since that statute of Magna Carta." [36] Already in 1606, Lord Chancellor Ellesmere, the report goes, "did likewise deliver that before Magna Charta was, the prerogative was; for Magna Charta is but a declaration or manifestation thereof. . . ." [37] These negative attitudes towards the Charter during James I's reign suggest that the Great Charter's effect on the formulation of constitutionalism may have been less real than apparent—perhaps even the product of retrospection. What truly counted in the long run were the patterns of procedure, within and without the doors of Parliament. The means used in the game of politics, in both palace and Parliament, and the principles devised to rationalize party positions, even more than Magna Carta eventually saved the subjects' liberties and established constitutionalism.

The more often men cited Magna Carta in Parliament, the more they distorted its original meaning, and the more they weakened its emotional appeal. At times their antics in the House of Commons reduced the Great Charter's role to something akin to comic opera. Such an occasion occurred in 1624 when Coryton in the House of Commons spoke for the Crown against another bill to observe Magna Carta. Paradoxically, he took the line that the terms of the bill to save the Charter were "contrary to the statute of Magna Carta," and a diarist recorded that "Mr. Coryton thinketh this bill crosseth the fourteenth chapter of Magna. Carta." [38] During the attempt to impeach the duke of Buckingham in 1626, the peer's friends—and, of course, his enemies— cited Magna Carta. The charges and retorts that Buckingham's opponents and his defenders bandied back and forth were not without humor. One member of the House of Commons, Mr. Whitacre, turned the tables on the duke's foes by quoting chapter 39 in Buckingham's defense and then concluding, in a diarist's terse prose: "the duke yet a free man; ought to be free till he have passed the judgement of his peers." [39]

The grand debates in the 1628 Parliament that produced the Petition of Right gave to Magna Carta an additional crowded hour of glorious life. When that Parliament had ended, the Great Charter's part in forming British constitutionalism was about played out. Ironically, the Great Charter was named three times in the Petition of Right where it remains enshrined—perhaps embalmed. Soon the Petition of Right itself superseded the Great Charter as a practical sanction and a political slogan for procuring the Englishman's rights and liberties. When Michael Sparke, a London publisher, cited Magna Carta before the court of high commission in 1629, he joined it to the Petition as ultimate authority, save for an express statute. Sparke protested that Queen Elizabeth's Star Chamber decree concerning censorship of the press ran "contrary to Magna Charta, the Petition of Right, and other statutes of this kingdom which no private decrees of any court of justice, but only an express act of parliament can control." [40] What jurists and statesmen now needed in order to resolve such conflicts in jurisdiction was either a constitution or a corpus of fundamental law. Back in 1596, Sir Francis Bacon's

Maxims of the Law used the word "fundamental" to mean "the basis of a constitution." He told how King Edward I—"bent himself to endow his state with sundry notable and fundamental laws, upon which the government ever since hath principally rested." [41] In a sense, Bacon was not far off the mark, for Edward I had made Magna Carta into common law and so an operative force in helping men to decide which laws to construe as fundamental. James I, too, believed in fundamental law, but to him it was a "law which amply supported the monarchy and kept subjects in their place." [42]

To convert this unfolding fundamental law into the concept of a constitution required the civil wars, the restoration of monarchy, and the Glorious Revolution. When all this had happened, the constitutional principles implicit in Magna Carta had far outrun its contents. Now and then politicians and pamphleteers would find the Great Charter useful, for it still carried an emotional impact of tradition, legend, and antiquity. Sir Edward Coke, through his *Institutes of the Laws of England,* had created a new myth and prepared Magna Carta for export overseas, and it soon became operative in another world. The Massachusetts General Court, already in 1635, had agreed that "some men should be appointed to frame a body of grounds of laws, in resemblance to a Magna Charta, which should be received for fundamental laws." [43] For England, the Great Charter would seem to have done its noblest work in helping men in their struggle to establish what Maitland called "the absolute supremacy of statute." The revolution of 1689 assured this, and with it ultimately the sovereignty of Parliament. True, Magna Carta had tagged along through the decades with the new constitutionalism; but by mid-century its *élan vital* was nearly spent. Oliver Cromwell did not conceal his contempt for the Charter. When the judges, "with all humility, mentioned the law and Magna Charta, Cromwell told them, with terms of contempt and derision," Lord Clarendon recorded, " 'their magna f—— should not control his actions; which he knew were for the safety of the Commonwealth.' "[44] Yet the Great Charter still stuck in the Protector's crop, and he found it a useful metaphor when talking about his never-ending search for a "final settlement," a constitution. In the Painted Chamber on September 12, 1654, Cromwell told members of his Parliament, "in every government there must be somewhat fundamental, somewhat like a Magna Charta, that should be standing and be unalterable." However, John Lilburne, that great Leveller, felt that "the greatest mischief of all and the oppressing bondage of England ever since the Norman yoke is a law called the common law." And to this remark he added, "Magna Charta itself being but a beggarly thing, containing many marks of intolerable bondage, and the laws that have been made since by parliaments have . . . made our governments much more oppressive and intolerable."[45]

Nevertheless, and perhaps quite naturally, the restoration of Charles II in 1660 brought with it a return to Magna Carta. Like other daughters of other revolutions, the Great Charter now became a champion of the establishment. It soon fell into the hands of country squires and justices of the peace, pompous windbags ardent to defend the re-establishment, who made of it a happy sanction of the *status quo ante bellum.* Especially valuable was the Charter's first chapter, the one that guaranteed the rights and privileges of the Church. One justice of the peace, Peniston Whalley, Esquire, printed his charge to the grand jury at Nottingham in April 1661, under the title *The Civil Rights and Conveniences of Episcopacy with the Inconveniences of Presbytery.* This squire quoted chapter 1 in its entirety; he then went on to describe the civil wars as "that great violation of Magna Charta," and he finally concluded with, "If Magna Charta be as most of us are apt to incline to believe, it is, like the laws of the Medes and Persians, unalterable." [46]

However, the Great Charter's role as rationalizer of things that were and of things yet to come, had not quite ended. An anonymous tract of 1683 that had been written in anticipation of the revolution of 1689 considered that Magna Carta contained fundamental law. Here, the author resurrected the old but useful formula that laws made contrary to the Charter were "adjudged to be void and of no effect." This same writer, moreover, went further still, over into the moral sphere, and he put the question, "whether any law be unjust or no, is to be decided by Magna Carta." [47] How badly men in the 1680s needed a constitution and how close they then were to making one!

After the flight of King James II and after William and Mary's accession in February 1689, many statements like Ferguson's *A Brief Justification of the Prince of Orange's Descent into England* appeared, and several of these tracts again carried allusions to the Great Charter. But by now, Magna Carta was only one of various historical precedents brought into play to justify the Glorious Revolution. William Atwood, in *The Fundamental Constitution of the English Government* (1690), for example, set forth the thesis that government originated in agreement, and he cited medieval statutes, Bracton, and Fleta to prove the existence of an original contract. Also, Atwood presented Magna Carta, its many confirmations, and the depositions of both Edward II and Richard II as precedents to prove that the English monarchy had been elective. For many a nascent constitutionalist, "no government is lawful but what is founded upon compact and agreement between those chosen to govern and those who condescend to be governed." [48] An anonymous pamphleteer, writing before July 1689, appealed to Magna Carta and declared: "therefore it is confirmed by lawyers and politicians that the reason of state is the rule and measure of all laws. Upon this account it is declared, that all acts and statutes shall be null which are contrary to Magna Charta and 42 Edward III, c. 1." [49] The very success of the 1689 revolution not only assured Britain of constitutionalism, and perhaps of a constitution too, but also secured the continuance of Magna Carta's golden legend. In England there remained the myth of Magna Carta to guide men in their quest for a constitution, a quest that still goes on.

Lest I now appear to have come to bury Magna Carta and not to praise it, let me try to put a fair and just value on the Great Charter's part in promoting constitutionalism. First of all, the Charter did help to stimulate and to sanction the formulation of the concept, the due process of law. It also preserved the medieval ideal of the law's supremacy and so promoted the principle of the rule of law. Furthermore, the fact of the Great Charter itself, following a century-old tradition of coronation charters—virtually, engagements between sovereign and subject—and the subsequent forty-four confirmations of the Charter, all these fostered the principle of contract, government by agreement. Also, the inviolability that men attributed to the Charter made of it a higher kind of law by which they might appraise the validity of ordinances and statutes. Thus Magna Carta, as a criterion of recognition of validity, inspired Englishmen eventually to create a set of principles that have assured the certainty in public law and the consistency in governance that form the quintessence of British constitutionalism.

No matter that the Petition of Right superseded Magna Carta as an operative idea in seventeenth-century constitutional conflicts; no matter that the Glorious Revolution and its settlement supplanted the Great Charter, at least among good Whigs, as a catchword to sanction party aspirations; and no matter that somber scholars, at Magna Carta's semi-centennial anniversaries, still go on chipping away the grandeur and the glory that Tudor and Stuart imaginations heaped upon the Charter. After all, the poets and the politicians have wrapped around Magna Carta myths that will continue to keep it a living idea. It is the first, the earliest of the four cornerstones upon which jurists and statesmen are still constructing British constitutionalism. "Magna Carta, the Petition of Right, and the Bill of Rights constitute, in the words of the elder Pitt, Lord Chatham, 'the Bible of the English Constitution.' " [50] To these three sacred sources may be added a fourth— one that Lord Chatham and his contemporaries around 1750 disclosed: "the spirit of the British Constitution." Since then statesmen and scholars, jurists and judges, divines and demagogues have defined, described, and disagreed about the nature of the Constitution's spirit. Blackstone before 1765 had found the essence of that spirit to be balance. To strike a balance between the governors and the governed was just what Magna Carta in 1215 had sought to do. Then for over four hundred years the Great Charter had helped to maintain a balance in governance, at times a most precarious one, by strengthening the two cardinal principles, contract and the rule of law. All along, men found in Magna Carta a sense of certainty that served them in place of a constitution. And so the very fact of Magna Carta, its existence, and its myth are likely to stand forth for centuries as the foursquare foundation underneath what Sir Edward Coke so happily styled, "the main pillars, and supporters of the fabric of the commonwealth." [51]

N O T E S

1 Horace Twiss, *Influence or Prerogative? Being an Attempt to Remove Certain Popular Misconceptions . . . the British Constitution and Government* (London, 1812), pp. 3-4.

2 "Constitution," "Constitutional," and "Constitutionalism," in *New English Dictionary on Historical Principles*. Constitution, *sub nomine,* does not appear in John Cowell, *The Interpreter of Words and Terms* (London, 1701), or in Giles Jacob, *A New Law-Dictionary* (London, 1736).

3 William H. Dunham, Jr., "Regal Power and the Rule of Law," *Journal of British Studies,* III (1964), 24-56.

4 William Blackstone, *Commentaries on the Laws of England* (London, 1809), Bk. I, Chap. 10, p. 370.

5 *The New York Times,* December 26, 1953, pp. 1, 6.

6 Frederick M. Powicke, *The Thirteenth Century* (Oxford, 1953), p. 536; Francis Palgrave, ed., *Parliamentary Writs,* I, 105, No. 45; William S. McKechnie, *Magna Carta* (Glasgow, 1914), pp. 506-7; 157. All references to the chapters of Magna Carta are to King John's Charter of 1215 as edited by McKechnie and numbered 1 to 63.

7 A. Luders, T. E. Tomlins, *et al.,* eds., *Statutes of the Realm* (London, 1810-28), I, 123.

8 *Idem,* p. 165. ". . . *si non en cas ou le roi poet faire grace solom son serment, e ceo par process de ley et la custume du realme. . . ."*

9 *Rotuli Parliamentorum* (London, 1832), II, 55, No. 13. ". . . *que come la Grant Chartre voet, que nul Comte, Baroun, ne nul autre du Roialme, soit jugge mes par proces de ses Peres. . . ."*

43

10 *Statutes of the Realm,* 25 Edward III, Statute 5, c. 4. The act *"acorde est, assenti et etabli";* and it named Magna Carta and included the clause *"sil ne soit par lei de la terre."*

11 *Idem,* I, 321.

12 *Rotuli Parliamentorum,* IV, 67, No. 9. The Sandwichers' petition ran: *"Plese à vous, honurables sires, considerer la matier suis dite, et auxi l'estatut del graunt chartre, qe fait mention qe null homme ne serroit jugge sinon par la commune ley, et auxi en autres estatutz d'auncien temps ordeignez, nully ne serroit moleste ne greve saunz due processe de ley. . . ."*

13 *Idem,* III, 417-22, Nos. 18-50.

14 Faith Thompson, *Magna Carta, Its Role in the Making of the English Constitution, 1300-1629* (Minneapolis, 1948), pp. 192, 194, quoting British Museum MS Harley 4990, fols. 154-79 (146-71).

15 *Idem,* pp. 284-93. Quotations on p. 288 from British Museum MS Harley 4841 (p. 285, n. 35).

16 *The Parliamentary or Constitutional History of England from the Earliest Times* . . . (London, 1751-62), II, 335.

17 *Rotuli Parliamentorum,* IV, 349, No. 5, par. 36.

18 John Foxe, *Acts and Monuments* (London, 1563), pp. 743, col. a, and 741, col. b.

19 William Roper, *The Life of Sir Thomas More,* R. S. Sylvester and D. P. Harding, eds. (New Haven, Conn., 1962), p. 249. *Statutes of the Realm,* 42 Edward III, c.1: it was "assented and accorded" that Magna Carta be kept, *"et si nul estatut soit fait à contraire soit tenuz pur nul";* H. S. Commager, *Documents of American History* (New York, 1934), p. 57.

20 William Caxton, *The Chronicles of England* (London, 1528, by Wynkyn de Worde), fol. lxxxviii, *recto* col. a and *verso* col. a.

21 Raphael Holinshed, *The Last Volume of the Chronicles of England, Scotland, and Ireland* (London, 1577), II, 626, 649.

22 William Lambarde, *Archeion,* C. H. McIlwain and Paul L. Ward, eds. (Cambridge, Mass., 1957), pp. 136-37.

23 Thompson, *Magna Carta,* p. 205 and n. 21, quoting British Museum MS Harley 6847, fol. 133-40.

24 *Idem,* pp. 219, 220, 222.

25 John E. Neale, *Elizabeth I and Her Parliaments, 1584-1601* (London, 1957), p. 231.

26 John Strype, *The Life and Acts of John Whitgift* (Oxford, 1822), I, 174.

27 *Idem,* II, 399.

28 Richard Cosin, *An Apologie for Sundrie Proceedings by Jurisdiction Ecclesiastical* (London, 1593), Pt. I, Chap. 14, pp. 102, 104.

29 *Idem,* p. 105.

30 James Spedding, ed., *The Letters and the Life of Francis Bacon* (London, 1868), IV, 350.

31 Thompson, *Magna Carta,* p. 284 and n. 33 ["Some notes and observations upon the Statute of Magna Carta . . . (collected by the Lord Ellesmere for the king's learned counsel's direction . . . September 1615 . . .)"]. No source or further reference appears.

32 *Idem,* p. 258, quoting British Museum MS Cotton, Cleopatra F II, fol. 191.

33 Edward Coke, *Reports,* II, vi-vii.

34 Thompson, *Magna Carta,* p. 258, quoting British Museum MS Cotton, Cleopatra F II, fol. 191.

35 Nicholas Fuller, *The Argvment of Master Nicholas Fvller, in the Case of Thomas Lad and Richard Mavnsell, his Clients . . . Imprinted 1607,* p. 5.

36 Thompson, *Magna Carta,* p. 263 and n. 83, quoting British Museum MS Cotton, Cleopatra F I, fols. 128-35 (127-34).

37 John Hawarde, *Les Reportes del Cases in Camera Stellata, 1593-1609,* W. P. Baildon, ed. (London, 1894), p. 278.

38 Thompson, *Magna Carta*, p. 313 and n. 59, quoting Sir Walter Erle's Diary (Gurney MS fol. 62 v).

39 *Idem*, p. 324, quoting Sir Richard Grosvenor's Diary of the 1626 Parliament.

40 *Idem*, p. 352, quoting *State Papers*, 16, 141/17, and described in *Calendar of State Papers, 1628-29*, p. 525.

41 Francis Bacon, *Maxims of the Law*, in *The Works of Francis Bacon*, James Spedding, ed. (London, 1859), VII, 314.

42 J. W. Gough, *Fundamental Law in English Constitutional History* (Oxford, 1955), p. 52.

43 *Winthrop's Journal: History of New England*, ed. J. K. Hosmer (New York, 1908), I, 151; *Records of the Governor and Company of Massachusetts Bay*, N. B. Shurtleff, ed., (Boston, 1853-1854), I, 147.

44 Edward Hyde, Earl of Clarendon, *The History of the Rebellion and Civil Wars in England* (Oxford, 1826), VII, 296.

45 C. H. Firth, ed., *The Clarke Papers*, Camden Soc., New Ser., xlix (Westminster, 1891), I, lxi, quoting John Lilburne, *Just Man's Justification*, pp. 11-15. W. C. Abbott, ed., *The Writings and Speeches of Oliver Cromwell* (Cambridge, Mass., 1945), III, 459. *Cf.* Clarendon, *History of the Rebellion and Civil Wars in England*, VII, 39: ". . . 'that in the government there were certain fundamentals, which could not be altered, to wit, that the government should be in a single person and a parliament; . . . that the militia should not be trusted into one hand, or power, but so as the parliament might have a check on the protector, and the protector on the parliament; that in matters of religion there ought to be a liberty of conscience, and that persecution in the church was not to be tolerated. These, he [Cromwell] said, were unalterable fundamentals. As for other things in the government, they were examinable and alterable as the state of affairs did require.' "

46 Thompson, *Magna Carta*, p. 372 and n. 44: "A printed tract of 13 pages, based on *State Papers*, 29, 34, no. 79."

47 Gough, *Fundamental Law in English Constitutional History*, p. 157, quoting an anonymous tract, *Fundamental Law the True Security of Sovereign Dignity and the People's Liberty*, 1683, p. 139.

48 *Idem*, p. 162, quoting Robert Ferguson, in *State Tracts* (London, 1689), I, 136; and p. 163, summarizing and quoting Atwood.

49 *A Brief Account of the Nullity of King James's Title . . .* (London, Licensed 27 July 1689, J. Fraser and printed for Richard Chiswell), p. 5.

50 Theodore F. T. Plucknett in T. P. Taswell-Langmead, *English Constitutional History* (Boston and London, 1946), p. 74.

51 Edward Coke, *Institutes of the Laws of England* (London, 1797), Vol. II, p. 74 (c. 35). Coke wrote, "so dangerous a thing it is to shake or alter any of the rules or fundamental points of the common law, which in truth are the main pillars, and supporters of the fabric of the commonwealth."

Magna Carta & Constitutionalism in the United States: "The Noble Lie"

Philip B. Kurland

One searches in vain among the leading casebooks from which American law students now learn their constitutional law for any reference to Magna Carta. Nor do the writings of political scientists and American constitutional historians reveal that Magna Carta is still viable. And if an examination of the decisions of the Supreme Court of the United States—that governmental body charged with keeping the American Constitution up to date—proves not quite so fruitless, it is hardly indicative of any great current vitality in the ancient scripture. Perhaps, then, at the age of seven hundred and fifty years, Magna Carta is deserving of no more in the United States than a quiet commemorative ceremony, a few short eulogies before it is permitted to return to its somnolence until the eight-hundredth anniversary calls for a similar ritual.

To speak of Magna Carta in this fashion, however, is to ignore its phoenixlike quality, its capacity for self-regeneration. The words of the late Sir Winston Churchill, himself an institution owed homage by the free world, are not inappropriate. Writing of Magna Carta, he stated:

> Now for the first time the King himself is bound by the law. . . . The Charter became in the process of time an enduring witness that the power of the Crown was not absolute.
>
> The facts embodied in it and the circumstances giving rise to them were buried or misunderstood. The underlying idea of the sovereignty of the law, long existent in feudal custom, was raised by it into a doctrine for the national State. And when in subsequent ages the State, swollen with its own authority, has attempted to ride roughshod over the rights or liberties of the subject it is to this doctrine that appeal has again and again been made, and never, as yet, without success.[1]

Churchillian—larger than life—prose is appropriate for description of Magna Carta because its utility in the constitutional domain has been so largely dependent upon its exaltation beyond the realm of fact.

It may be for this reason—because Magna Carta in American constitutionalism has played essentially the role that would have been served in Plato's *Republic* by the "noble lie"—that students of the American Constitution have left to historians the contest over the accuracy of description of the events that transpired at Runnymede three quarters of a millennium ago. The place of Magna Carta in American constitutional development, past and future, is not dependent on whether Hume[2] and Radin[3] rather than Hegel[4] and Jenks[5] were right about the contemporaneous meaning of the agreement between King John and his recalcitrant barons. For Magna Carta, in American constitutional development, has proved Carlyle's dictum that "in every object there is

49

inexhaustible meaning; the eye sees in it what the eye brings means of seeing." [6]

This equanimity about the truth or falsehood of the origins of Magna Carta may also be due to the fact that America's inheritance of the doctrines allegedly contained therein was by way of the stewardship of Sir Edward Coke. Those who look kindly on Coke's contribution may accept the judgment of Britain's foremost scholar on Magna Carta. About half a century ago, William Sharp McKechnie wrote: "If the vague and inaccurate words of Coke have obscured the bearing of many chapters [of Magna Carta], and diffused false notions of the development of English law, the service these very errors have done to the cause of constitutional progress is measureless." [7] To a generation for which the notion of the "discovery" of law by judges has largely been replaced by a recognition that judicial doctrine is created rather than inspired, Professor Max Radin's evaluation of the Coke contribution is more readily acceptable:

> The authority of Coke's writings was so great that for many purposes, his statements are a point of departure for the Common Law from the seventeenth century on. This is of particular importance for the development of American law, since most men neither had the desire nor the facilities to go behind Coke in order to determine whether his dogmatic statements about the Common Law were well-founded. Even his historical errors became accepted—his absurd claims for the antiquity of the Common Law, his complete misunderstanding of Magna Carta, his uncritical acceptance of ancient forgeries like the "Mirror of Justices." He created for later generations not only the "myth of Magna Carta" but the much more deleterious myth of the Common Law as a complete system "locked in the breasts of the judges," who by a mystical but not specified process declare law without making it. [8]

Thus, though Americans, like Englishmen, must join in Trevelyan's dictum: "The first great step on the constitutional road was Magna Carta," [9] perhaps the historic date for the United States should be regarded, not as 1215, but as 1606, when the Virginia Charter was penned in part by Sir Edward Coke, Attorney-General to King James, or perhaps 1628, when the Second Part of Coke's *Institutes*—his commentary on Magna Carta—was completed, or even 1642, when this portion of the *Institutes* was published. For American history has made clear that it was not the treaty between John and the barons at Runnymede that provided "the first great step on the constitutional road," but Coke's version thereof, especially when combined with his equally inaccurate but highly palatable conception of the common law.

The relevance of the Virginia Charter derives from its provision that the colonists in this domain of the Crown were to be regarded as Englishmen who "shall HAVE and enjoy all Liberties, Franchises, and Immunities, within any of our other Dominions, to all Intents and Purposes, as if they had been abiding and born, within this our Realm of *England,* or any other of our said Dominions." Language of similar effect was included in the later charters: the Charter of New England, 1620; the Charter of Massachusetts Bay, 1629; the Charter of Maryland, 1632; the Charter of Maine, 1639; the Charter of Connecticut, 1662; the Charter of Rhode Island, 1663; the Charter of Carolina, 1663; and the Charter of Georgia, 1732.[10] The charters gave the rights of Englishmen; Coke's interpretation of the rights of Englishmen afforded by Magna Carta, therefore, proved most congenial to the new American climate.

At this point it should be noted that two of the most important contributions of Magna Carta to American constitutionalism were implicit rather than explicit in that document, even with the transmutations that Coke made. The first of these is that Magna Carta has been considered—whatever the facts—to be the beginning in Anglo-American history of the idea of a hierarchy of laws, an idea that is of the very essence of constitutionalism. The second is that Magna Carta represents the utilization of a written document as the guide to, if not the encompassment of, the highest law within the hierarchy of laws. Indeed, it is this second factor that primarily distinguishes American constitutionalism from its English brother. (I am not speaking here of the actual novelty of the Charter as written law. I suggest only the repeated attribution of this concept to Magna Carta in American history.)

That fundamental legal principles should be reduced to writing soon became a precept of government in the American colonies. Hard on the heels of the royal charters, in which the power of local legislation was also granted, came the many attempts of the new dominions to establish by their own written laws their claims to the rights of Englishmen—not the least of which were those contained in Magna Carta. Thus, in the Massachusetts colony, the first legislation passed was its "Body of Liberties" of 1641, a curious conglomeration of theocratic principles joined with those of the common law. The first two sections of the "Body of Liberties" were derived directly from chapters 39 and 40 of Magna Carta. And when the time came to revise this legislation, the Massachusetts General Court, in order to accomplish this purpose, sent to England for two copies of Sir Edward Coke's commentaries on Magna Carta, among a few other law tomes.[11] The result was that in the second version of the Massachusetts legislation, Holy Writ played a smaller part and Magna Carta a larger one. The example set by Massachusetts was soon followed in the New Haven Code of 1656, the Charter of Fundamental Law of West New Jersey of 1677, the New York Charter of Liberties of 1683, the South Carolina Act of 1712, and the North Carolina Act of 1715.

The Rhode Island charter, with Roger Williams as its guiding spirit, eschewed all use of the Holy Word in favor of chapter 39 of Magna Carta. "Williams believed in a variety of natural rights, derived rationally from the character of natural law. Religious liberty was one of these. . . . Government must guarantee liberty of persons, by which he meant freedom from arbitrary punishment or restraint, and liberty of 'estates,' by which he meant right of property." [12]

Pennsylvania's Charter of Privileges of 1682 directly reflected William Penn's familiarity with Coke and Magna Carta, a familiarity he had demonstrated in 1670 at Old Bailey when he challenged the indictment pending against him on the basis of law stated in Coke's *Second Institutes*.[13] This reliance was again revealed in Penn's pamphlet in 1675, entitled *England's Present Interest*,[14] in which he asserted the rights of colonials as Englishmen protected by Magna Carta, as construed by Coke.

The assertion of such rights by the colonists did not meet with uniform approval in the mother country, especially immediately after the English revolution of 1688, when the claim to the rights of Englishmen in the New York Charter of Privileges and Liberties and the Maryland Assembly's adoption of Magna Carta were vetoed by the Crown because of inconsistency with the royal prerogative. In keeping with the spirit and position of their tutor, Sir Edward Coke, the colonists of this day were still asserting the supremacy of Parliament. It was not until a later day in American history that Coke's teachings of the supremacy of the common law, even over Parliament, were to take effect. Thus, Wright finds in the *Declaration of the Gentlemen, Merchants, and Inhabitants of Boston,* one of the *Andros Tracts* published in 1689, a defense of the colonists' "claim to the rights of Englishmen by appeal to their charter, to Magna Charta, and to Common Law. Unlike their descendants," Wright says, "they stress rights and privileges of Parliament as against the prerogative." [15] As late as 1728, when Daniel Dulany, the Attorney-General of Maryland, contested the power of the Crown to reject the adoption of English statutes by the Maryland legislature, the issue was framed in terms of parliamentary supremacy, still relying on Coke and Magna Carta.[16]

It is not yet clear, because of the absence of adequate scholarly treatment of the early law reports, whether Magna Carta played an important role in the decisions of lawsuits during this colonial period. It was anticipated by Hazeltine "that colonial case-law will be found, on examination, to embody principles of Magna Carta." He relied in part on "the well-known fact that in judicial proceedings of the period parties frequently claimed the rights of 'every free born English subject.' " [17]

Certainly it is true that during the Revolutionary period Magna Carta was the frequent basis for claim of right against the English government, both in litigation and in political tracts. To cite but a few examples, Andrew Hamilton's defense of Peter Zenger's right to freedom of the press was based on Coke and Magna Carta, and James Otis' famed *Rights of the American Colonies* of 1764 was similarly buttressed. Thomas Hutchinson, committed foe of John Adams and James Otis, in speaking in 1765 against the Stamp Tax, said: "The prevailing reason . . . is that the act of Parliament is against Magna Charta and the natural rights of Englishmen [and] according to Lord Coke, null and void." [18] Even that battlecry of the American Revolution, "No taxation without representation," allegedly derived from Magna Carta. As Becker put it:

> . . . the colonists seized upon the well-established tradition that British liberty had originally been won, and had always been maintained, by a stubborn and persistent parliamentary opposition to arbitrary taxation. This opposition, as a matter of sober historical fact, had never been more than intermittently effective until the seventeenth century; but the parliamentary

party of that time, in defense of *their* rights, maintained that parliamentary control of taxation was as old as Magna Carta. And so in the eighteenth century it was commonly accepted as a principle of the British Constitution that no Englishman could be legally taxed, except by his own consent, that is, by his representative in Parliament.[19]

Indeed, the very right of revolution is to be found in the interstices of Magna Carta. In speaking of that document's defects, McKechnie suggests that "instead of constitutional machinery to turn the theories of Magna Carta into realities, 'a right of legalized rebellion' was conferred on an executive committee of twenty-five of the King's enemies." [20]

If by the time the seeds of the American Revolution were being sown a doctrinal shift away from the positivistic search for language in English statutes to the more amorphous notions of natural rights had taken place, there was no need to abandon reliance on Magna Carta. Its capacities for adaptation having been demonstrated in its utilization to support the legislature against the Crown, although it originated in a contest between the barons and the king, Magna Carta was ready to take on a new form as essential proof of the natural law that attested the rights of the people against government, including the legislative branch. Thus, we are informed by Max Weber, in speaking of the origins of natural law:

> To some extent, it is derived, too, from the idea, particularly indigenous to England, that every member of the community has certain inherent natural rights. This specifically English concept of "birthright" arose essentially under the influence of the popular conception that certain rights, which had been confirmed in Magna Carta as the special status rights of the barons, were national liberties of all Englishmen as such and that they were thus immune against any interference by the King or any other political authority.[21]

The tradition of Magna Carta did not die with the separation of the several states from the mother country. Americans now, the former colonials still coveted the rights of Englishmen, especially as those rights were romanticized in the myths of Magna Carta. Despite the newly dominant concept of natural rights as described in the Declaration of Independence, the people of each state secured, in the image of the Great Charter, a written constitution limiting the powers to be exercised over them by the governments that they thereby created. And into each of these state constitutions crept the very language of Magna Carta. Thus, as Lord Bryce said: "The Bill of Rights is historically the most interesting part of these Constitutions, for it is the legitimate child and representative of Magna Charta, and of those other declarations and enactments . . . by which the liberties of Englishmen have been secured. Most of the thirteen colonies when they asserted their independence and framed their Constitutions inserted a declaration of the fundamental rights of the people, and the example then set has been followed by the newer States." [22] And of all of Magna Carta's chapters, the thirty-ninth was the one that was included, *mutatis mutandis,* in each of them.

One interesting fact to note is that, despite the position taken by Coke in *Bonham's Case*[23] and elsewhere, suggesting the power of a court to hold legislation invalid because it contravened "higher law," "not one [of the new state constitutions] made any provision for judicial review" [24] as a means of assuring compliance with the fundamental law.

When the time came to frame the national Constitution, the same process was repeated, but in two steps rather than one. The primary weakness of the national Constitution as first promulgated was its failure to enumerate the rights of the people against the central government in the fashion of Magna Carta and successive documents that formed part of the English Constitution. This deficiency, which had threatened the very adoption of the federal Constitution, was remedied almost immediately by the enactment of ten amendments, the first eight of which have since been referred to as the Bill of Rights. Thus, the national Constitution, like those of the states, contains within it a large number of fundamental principles derived—immediately or ultimately—from Magna Carta as it was read by the American citizenry of the late eighteenth century, that is to say, as it was read by Coke.

It is hardly feasible here to elucidate each of the provisions of the American Constitution that find some basis in Magna Carta. Suffice it for our purposes to suggest a few, with recognition that the language and problems of feudal England were somewhat different from those of the emerging nation. Thus, in both documents are provision for freedom of the Church; expression of limitations tending toward the establishment of an independent judiciary; provision for limiting venue for certain actions; limitations on taking of private property and provision for payment therefor; requirement of speedy trial; and requirement that evidence be adduced before a charge may be preferred against a defendant. But clearly the most important provision of Magna Carta insofar as the Constitution of the United States is concerned is chapter 39, which reads: "No freeman shall be taken or imprisoned or disseised or exiled or in any way destroyed, nor will we go upon him nor send upon him, except by the lawful judgment of his peers or by the law of the land." It is the relevance of this clause to the development of constitutional doctrine on which I would dwell, but first I would remind you not of what was old in the American Constitution but rather of what was new.

The novelty of the American Constitution—whether intended or not is still a matter of controversy—is to be found in the allocation to the judiciary of the power to restrain government action contravening the fundamental law. No longer were the people to be dependent upon the self-restraint of the legislature for assurance of the guarantees of freedom. The legislative supremacy Magna Carta had helped impose on the Crown in the seventeenth century was supplanted in the New World by judicial supremacy over the meaning of the fundamental law. For this reason the importance of Magna Carta to American constitutionalism is, from that point on, to be discovered in judicial opinions rather than legislative acts or political tracts. Moreover, since the Supreme Court in time became dominant in the formulation of constitutional doctrine, one must look to that Court's judgments to discover the transmission to the United States of the protection of the thirty-ninth chapter of Magna Carta.

At the time in our history when the Supreme Court took over the job of interpreting and applying the language of the Constitution derived from Magna Carta, the inheritance from that document in its most expansive form might be summarized thus: First, Magna Carta stood for the concept of the sovereign power of the people to impose their will on government, so that government became the servant rather than the master of the people. Second, Magna Carta stood for the notion that the expression of the will of the people about the fundamental rights that were retained by them was to be itemized in a written document. Third, Magna Carta stood for the idea that the written document would be superior to the legislative power as well as the executive power, a departure from its interpretation in England, if not from that interpretation which Lord Coke had unsuccessfully attempted to impose on English law. Fourth, Magna Carta stood for the proposition that the written document, though specifying the limits of governmental power, was merely a recording of rights that existed prior to the promulgation of the charter and, insofar as the writing was deficient in stating all those rights, those not stated were nonetheless retained. This last proposition was specifically written into the American Constitution in the Ninth Amendment, which provides: "The enumeration in the Constitution of certain rights, shall not be construed to deny or discharge others retained by the people." The Ninth Amendment has been properly described as the "forgotten" amendment of the Constitution. I believe, however, that it has before it a great future which will unfold in the coming decades and which will, initially, be based on legitimation by Magna Carta. But our immediate concern here is not with the Ninth Amendment, which derives from no specific language of Magna Carta, but with the due process clauses of the Fifth and Fourteenth Amendments, whose parentage in that document has been determined beyond doubt.

This portion of the Supreme Court's history starts not with interpretation of the provisions of the national Constitution, however, but rather with the Constitution of the State of Maryland, which used, instead of the phrase "due process of law," the very words of the Charter, "law of the land." In *Bank of Columbia v. Okley,* in 1819, Mr. Justice Johnson said: "As to the words of Magna Carta, incorporated into the constitution of Maryland, after volumes spoken and written with a view to their exposition, the good sense of mankind has at length settled down to this: that they were intended to secure the individual from the arbitrary exercise of the powers of government, unrestrained by the established principles of private rights and distributive justice." [25] It was, I submit, hardly useful to translate "law of the land" into "established principles of private rights and distributive justice" if what was intended was a guide to judicial decision. It was more likely to afford judicial discord than judicial restraint. And this could hardly have been the intent of a Justice who, in a concurring opinion some years later, announced: "Courts of justice are properly excluded from all considerations of policy, and therefore are very unfit instruments to control the action of that branch of government which may often be compelled by the highest considerations of public policy to withhold even the exercise of a positive duty." [26] But before we condemn Johnson for his failure to provide adequate guidelines for the meaning of due process, it should be recognized that the intervening decades have not provided us with any more certain a measure than "established principles of private right and distributive justice."

Johnson's definition may have been a reflection of that which was offered the Court by Daniel Webster in his argument in the *Dartmouth College Case*,[27] which, though not taken up by the Court at that time, did have a widespread influence among state courts and commentators. Webster had contended:

> By the law of the land is most clearly intended the general law; a law which hears before it condemns; which proceeds upon inquiry, and renders judgment only after trial. The meaning is, that every citizen shall hold his life, liberty, property, and immunities under the protection of the general rules which govern society. Every thing which may pass under the form of an enactment is not therefore to be considered the law of the land. If this were so, acts of attainder, bills of pains and penalties, acts of confiscation, acts reversing judgments, and acts directly transferring one man's estate to another, legislative judgments, decrees, and forfeitures in all possible forms, would be the law of the land.
>
> Such a construction would render constitutional provisions of the highest importance completely inoperative and void. It would tend directly to establish the union of all powers in the legislature. There would be no general, permanent law for courts to administer or men to live under. The administration of jus-

tice would be an empty form, an idle ceremony. Judges would sit to execute legislative judgments and decrees; not to declare the law or administer the justice of the country.[28]

Webster's argument would have gladdened the soul of Sir Edward Coke, as it was to warm the cockles of the hearts of American corporations in future years. But it did not take hold in the Court to begin with, perhaps because the Supreme Court's interpretation of the due process clause of the Fifth Amendment was not forthcoming until *Murray's Lessee v. Hoboken Land & Improvement Co.,*[29] in 1855. Mr. Justice Curtis, the author of that opinion, was one of the most learned lawyers ever to attain a seat on the high court. He had, long before his arrival at that tribunal, demonstrated his familiarity with Magna Carta and Coke's *Institutes.* His notions of Magna Carta were a bit romantic. He regarded it as an "affirmance of the ancient standing laws of the land, as they had existed among the Saxons ere the power of Norman chivalry, combined with the subtlety of Norman lawyers, had deprived the Saxons—who then formed, and whose descendants still form, the mass of the English nation—of their ancient civil and political institutions." [30] For him it was, indeed, an expansive document. As a lawyer he found propositions in Magna Carta that it is difficult for others to see. Thus, he argued that the power to punish for contempt of court was of "immemorial usage and recognized by Magna Carta itself," but here he really was relying on Blackstone.[31] In the role of jurist he was more circumspect in his interpretation. As a United States circuit judge, he interpreted the language of the Rhode Island Constitution, which had used the words of Magna Carta, the "law of the land," saying: "The exposition of these words as they stand in Magna Carta, as well as in the American Constitutions, has been that they require 'due process of law'; and in this is necessarily implied and included the right to answer to and contest the charge, and the consequent right to be discharged from it, unless it is proved. Lord Coke, giving the interpretation of these words in Magna Carta (*Institutes,* II, 50, 51), says they mean due process of law, in which is included presentment or indictment, and being brought in to answer thereto. And the jurists of our country have not relaxed this interpretation." [32]

When he came to write the opinion for the Supreme Court in the case of *Murray's Lessee,* he again wrote in terms of procedural safeguards. The case raised the issue of the validity of a sale of property by the solicitor of the treasury pursuant to a warrant authorized to be issued by Congressional legislation of 1820. The Court was put to answer the question whether such summary procedure complied with the requirements of "due process of law." After identifying "due process of law" with the phrase "law of the land," by reference to Coke, Curtis proceeded:

That the warrant now in question is legal process, is not denied. It was issued in conformity with an act of Congress. But is it "due process of law"? The constitution contains no description of those processes which it was intended to allow or forbid. It does not even declare what principles are to be applied to ascertain whether it be due process. It is manifest that it was not left to the legislative power to enact any process which might be devised. The article is a restraint on the legislative as well as on the executive and judicial powers of the government, and cannot be so construed as to leave congress free to make any process "due process of law," by its mere will. To what principles, then, are we to resort to ascertain whether this process, enacted by congress, is due process? To this the answer must be twofold. We must examine the constitution itself, to see whether this process be in conflict with any of its provisions. If not found to be so, we must look to those settled usages and modes of proceeding existing in the common and statue [sic] law of England, before the emigration of our ancestors, and which are shown not to have been unsuited to their civil and political condition by having been acted upon by them after the settlement of this country.[33]

After extensive examination of history, Curtis sustained the summary procedure devised by Congress to effectuate collection of its debts.

Three points about this opinion should be noted. First, the due process clause was held binding on Congress in that "due process of law" did not mean merely process according to the prescription of the legislature. Second, the due process clause was in fact concerned with procedure, a point that might seem apparent from the words but which the Court was shortly thereafter to abandon. Third, the valid process was held to be that which could be justified in terms of history, a construction that might have severely limited the growth of the due process clause.

In the words of Haines: "Due Process is at this stage familiar, or more accurately, common-law process. But the modern development has been a by-product of judicial concern with the protection of property and individual rights from interference by the federal government." [34]

The Magna Carta as guide to the meaning of the due process clause of the Fourteenth Amendment, as distinguished from the Fifth, was revealed in 1877 in *Davidson v. New Orleans*.[35] But this time, not even so clear an answer as that afforded by Mr. Justice Curtis was forthcoming. Mr. Justice Miller, after also attributing the origins of the clause to Magna Carta, stated:

> It must be confessed, however, that the constitutional meaning or value of the phrase "due process of law," remains to-day without that satisfactory precision of definition which judicial decisions have given to nearly all the other guarantees of personal rights found in the constitutions of the several States and of the United States.[36]

The Court was still in agreement that the limitation was on the legislature as well as the executive:

> It is easy to see that when the great barons of England wrung from King John, at the point of the sword, the concession that neither their lives nor their property should be disposed of by the crown, except as provided by the law of the land, they meant by "law of the land" the ancient and customary laws of the English people, or laws enacted by the Parliament of which those barons were a controlling element.[37]

(Mr. Justice Miller would have been hard put to discover legislation of the English Parliament of this period. As McIlwain said: "In mediaeval England legislation in its proper sense was all but unknown. Laws in feudal times are in the main declarations of existing custom; they are as Professor Jenks says, 'not enactments, but records.' " [38] But then it has long been the custom of Justices of the Supreme Court of the United States to rewrite history rather freely.[39])

> It was not in their minds [Mr. Justice Miller continued], therefore, to protect themselves against the enactments of the laws by the Parliament of England. But when, in the year of grace 1866, there is placed in the Constitution of the United States a declaration that "no State shall deprive any person of life, liberty, or property without due process of law," can a State make any thing due process of law which, by its own legislation, it chooses to declare such? To affirm this is to hold that the prohibition to the States is of no avail, or has no application where the invasion of private rights is effected under the terms of state legislation.[40]

Miller went on to disparage the function of the due process clause as a general license to the Court to oversee state and federal legislation:

It is not a little remarkable, that while this provision has been in the Constitution of the United States, as a restraint upon the authority of the Federal government, for nearly a century, and while, during all that time, the manner in which the powers of that government have been exercised has been watched with jealousy, and subjected to the most rigid criticism in all its branches, this special limitation upon its powers has rarely been invoked in the judicial forum or the more enlarged theatre of public discussion. But while it has been a part of the Constitution, as a restraint upon the power of the States, only a very few years, the docket of this court is crowded with cases in which we are asked to hold that State courts and State legislatures have deprived their own citizens of life, liberty, or property without due process of law. There is here abundant evidence that there exists some strange misconception of the scope of this provision as found in the fourteenth amendment. In fact, it would seem, from the character of the many cases before us, and the arguments made in them, that the clause under consideration is looked upon as a means of bringing to the test of the decision of this court the abstract opinions of every unsuccessful litigant in a State court of the justice of the decision against him, and of the merits of the legislation on which such a decision may be founded.[41]

He concluded by adhering to the view that the guarantee of the due process clause was limited to procedural safeguards:

. . . it is not possible to hold that a party has, without due process of law, been deprived of his property, when, as regards the issues affecting it, he has, by the laws of the State, a fair trial in a court of justice, according to the modes of proceeding applicable to such a case.[42]

Mr. Justice Bradley, concurring, was not satisfied with quite so limited a form of review. But neither was he at that time prepared to broaden the notion to that which so many litigants were already urging on the Court:

I think . . . we are entitled, under the fourteenth amendment, not only to see that there is some process of law, but "due process of law," provided by the state law when a citizen is deprived of his property; and that, in judging what is "due process of law," respect must be had to the cause and object of the taking, whether under the taxing power, the power of eminent domain, or the power of assessment for local improvements, or none of these: and if found to be suitable or admissible in the special case, it will be adjudged to be "due process of law"; but if found to be arbitrary, oppressive, and unjust, it may be declared to be not "due process of law." Such an examination may be made without interfering with that large discretion which every legislative power has of making wide modifications in the forms of procedure in each case, according as the laws, habits, customs, and preferences of the people of the particular State may require.[43]

Justices Miller and Bradley were still talking only of procedure, but the historical measure seems to have been implicitly abandoned.

It was explicitly abandoned in the third of the four major Supreme Court decisions concerned with the relation of Magna Carta to the due process clause. In the case of *Hurtado v. California*,[44] a judicial debate between Mr. Justice Matthews, for the majority, and Mr. Justice Harlan, in dissent, was concerned with the proper meaning of "due process of law" as derived from Magna Carta. The majority in *Hurtado* rejected Mr. Justice Curtis' proposition that history was to be the measure of procedural due process. In thus sanctioning the State's abandonment of the grand jury indictment in capital cases, the Court returned to Mr. Justice Johnson's definition in *Okely*. And speaking of Curtis' decision in *Murray's Lessee*, Matthews said:

The real syllabus of the passage quoted is, that a process of law, which is not otherwise forbidden, must be taken to be due process of law, if it can show the sanction of settled usage both in

England and in this country; but it by no means follows that nothing else can be due process of law. The point in the case cited arose in reference to a summary proceeding, questioned on that account as not due process of law. The answer was: however exceptional it may be, as tested by definitions and principles of ordinary procedure, nevertheless, this, in substance, has been immemorially the actual law of the land, and, therefore, is due process of law. But to hold that such a characteristic is essential to due process of law, would be to deny every quality of law but its age, and to render it incapable of progress or improvement. It would be to stamp upon our jurisprudence the unchangeableness attributed to the laws of the Medes and Persians.[45]

Mr. Justice Harlan found it difficult, especially in a capital case, to discover the benefits of the novelty of dispensing with grand jury indictment in favor of an information filed by a prosecutor. Both majority and minority in *Hurtado* canvassed English and American legal history extensively in reaching their respective conclusions.

The destruction of the limited nature of "due process of law" in procedural matters came in *Twining v. New Jersey*.[46] It was in this case that a different form of test was originated, somewhat similar to that of Mr. Justice Johnson in *Okely*. Having decided that under Curtis' test New Jersey was not required to afford defendants the privilege against self-crimination because historically that right did not exist, the Court went on to "modernize" its rule:

. . . without repudiating or questioning the test proposed by Mr. Justice Curtis for the court, or rejecting the inference drawn from English law, we prefer to rest our decision on broader grounds and inquire whether the exemption from self-crimination is of such a nature that it must be included in the concept of due process. Is it a fundamental principle of liberty and justice which inheres in the very idea of free government and is the

inalienable right of a citizen of such government? If it is, and
if it is of a nature that pertains to process of law, this court has
declared it to be essential to due process of law. In approaching
such a question it must not be forgotten that in a free representative government nothing is more fundamental than the right of
the people through their appointed servants to govern themselves in accordance with their own will, except so far as they
have restrained themselves by constitutional limits specifically
established, and that in our peculiar dual form of government
nothing is more fundamental than the full power of the State
to order its own affairs and govern its own people, except so far
as the Federal Constitution expressly or by fair implication has
withdrawn that power.[47]

Again Mr. Justice Harlan was in dissent. And, while it is true that
in 1964 the Supreme Court overruled the decision in *Twining*
that the privilege against self-crimination was not guaranteed by
the Fourteenth Amendment's due process clause,[48] the Court has
not yet withdrawn from the definition of due process as rephrased
by Mr. Justice Cardozo in *Palko v. Connecticut*,[49] that due process
of law includes only those things that are of the very essence "of a
scheme of ordered liberty."

From Mr. Justice Johnson's "principles of private rights and
distributive justice" to Mr. Justice Cardozo's "scheme of ordered
liberty" as a definition of procedural due process of law certainly
comes close to being a complete circle. And it should be pointed
out that in the interim a circle within the circle was also almost
completed which affected the Court's ultimate choice of a license
to itself to sit in judgment on the action of state and national
legislatures and executives in procedural matters. Shortly after
Mr. Justice Miller's rejection, in *Davidson,* of the "strange misconception" that "the clause under consideration . . . [is] a
means of bringing to the test of the decision of this court [by]
every unsuccessful litigant in a State court of the justice of the

decision against him, and of the merits of the legislation on which such decision may be founded," the Supreme Court began to use the clause for that very purpose. Indeed, the origins of such "substantive due process," as it became known, may be traced to the infamous decision in *Dred Scott v. Sanford,*[50] where Mr. Chief Justice Taney announced: ". . . the rights of property are united with the rights of person, and placed on the same ground by the Fifth Amendment to the Constitution, which provides that no person shall be deprived of life, liberty, and property, without due process of law. And an Act of Congress which deprives a citizen of the United States of his liberty or property"—the property of which he was speaking was a slave—"merely because he came himself or brought his property into a particular Territory of the United States, and who had committed no offence against the laws, could hardly be dignified with the name of due process of law." However valid this attribution, in a long series of cases following *Davidson,* none of which seems to have placed reliance on the antecedent of Magna Carta, the Court was asked to and did pass on the desirability of legislation, both state and federal. "Substantive due process" flourished in the late nineteenth and early twentieth centuries as the Court placed stringent limitations on legislative power in the regulation of economic affairs. The exercise of this power reached its heights in the 1930s and subsided only after President Roosevelt's court-packing plan was submitted to Congress.

The strange notion abounds that substantive due process is dead. But the fact is that only in the area of economic regulation—if there—is it moribund.[51] In other areas, the Justices of the Supreme Court continue to exercise, under the aegis of the due process clauses, a veto power, wrapped, as Judge Learned Hand said, "in a protective veil of adjectives such as 'arbitrary,' 'artificial,' 'normal,' 'reasonable,' 'inherent,' 'fundamental,' or 'essential,' whose office usually, though quite innocently, is to disguise what they are doing and impute to it a derivation far more impressive than their personal preferences, which are all that in fact lie behind the decision." [52]

The contemporary conflict over the meaning of the Fourteenth Amendment's due process clause, between the "strict constructionists" who would allegedly limit its meaning to the guarantees contained in the first eight amendments and those who would continue to speak in terms of Cardozo's concept of "ordered liberty," is not within the scope of this discussion. The immediate influence of Magna Carta is not to be seen in the opposing arguments over this issue. But this point in the development of the concept of "due process of law" is not untypical of the influence of Magna Carta on American constitutionalism. In the due process clauses, as elsewhere, Magna Carta provided the starting point for the framing of standards appropriate to the safeguarding of liberties of a people living under a regime socially, economically, and politically about as far from that of 1215 as it is possible to conceive. Having served its function of putting the law on the right track, Magna Carta receded into the background. But it is to be expected that if the due process clauses become stultified in effectuating the liberties of the people, the courts will turn back to Magna Carta, either to initiate the use of another provision of the Constitution, like the Ninth Amendment, or to put the due process clauses themselves back on the proper road. In the interim, Magna Carta will be kept alive by the Court by infrequent references such as that of Mr. Justice Frankfurter in *Bridges v. California*[53] where he said: "The administration of justice by an impartial judiciary has been basic to our conception of freedom ever since Magna Carta." A still more recent example is that of Mr. Justice Goldberg, who, in his opinion in *Kennedy v. Mendoza-Martinez*,[54] opined: "Dating back to Magna Carta, however, it has been an abiding principle governing the lives of civilized men that 'no freeman shall be taken or imprisoned or disseissed or outlawed or exiled . . . without judgment of his peers or by the law of the land. . . .'" Obviously both Justices were indulging in hyperbole. But such is the power still attributed to Magna Carta, 750 years after King John met the barons at Runnymede, that both Justices Frankfurter and Goldberg apparently were of the belief that legitimacy was lent to their views by the incantation of the magic words.

And this, at last, brings me back to my starting point. Magna Carta's specific influence on current American constitutional doctrine is difficult to discover. Yet, unlike the common law with which Coke would have equated it, it does remain "a brooding omnipresence in the sky" of a society that has long recognized the great values of "legalism."[55] Magna Carta continues to be the prime symbol of the goal of Anglo-American constitutionalism: "freedom under law." No more should be asked of it.

N O T E S

1 Winston S. Churchill, *A History of the English-Speaking Peoples* (New York, 1956), I, 257.

2 David Hume, *History of Great Britain* (London, 1776), I, 444-45.

3. Max Radin, "The Myth of Magna Carta," *Harvard Law Review,* LX (1947), 1060.

4 G. W. F. Hegel, *Lectures on the Philosophy of History*, tr. J. Sibree (New York, 1956), p. 430.

5 Edward Jenks, "The Myth of Magna Carta," *Independent Review*, IV (1904), 260.

6 Thomas Carlyle, *History of the French Revolution*, Pt. I, Bk. i, Chap. 2.

7 William S. McKechnie, *Magna Carta* (2d ed.; Glasgow, 1914), p. 133.

8 Max Radin, *Handbook of Anglo-American Legal History* (St. Paul, Minn., 1936), p. 286. But see Faith Thompson, *Magna Carta, Its Role in the Making of the English Constitution, 1300-1629* (Minneapolis, 1948), p. 356.

9 G. M. Trevelyan, *History of England* (3d ed.; Garden City, N.Y., 1953), I, 227.

10 The charters and other colonial documents referred to in this essay are all to be found in Francis Newton Thorpe, ed., *The Federal and State Constitutions, Colonial Charters, and Other Organic Laws* (Washington, D.C., 1909).

11 Charles M. Andrews, *The Colonial Period of American History* (New Haven, Conn., 1934), I, 457.

12 Alfred H. Kelly and Winfred A. Harbison, *The American Constitution* (3d ed.; New York, 1963), p. 43.

13 *Selected Works of William Penn* (3d ed.; London, 1782), III, 218-19.

14 *Idem,* p. 202.

15 Benjamin F. Wright, *American Interpretations of Natural Law* (Cambridge, Mass., 1931), p. 38.

16 Daniel Dulany, Sr., *The Right of the Inhabitants of Maryland to the Benefit of the English Laws* (Annapolis, Md., 1728).

17 H. D. Hazeltine, "The Influence of Magna Carta on American Constitutional Development," *Columbia Law Review*, I (1917), 17.

18 Quoted in Roscoe Pound, *The Development of Constitutional Guarantees of Liberty* (New Haven, Conn., 1957), p. 79.

19 Carl L. Becker, *The Declaration of Independence* (New York, 1942), pp. 85-86.

20 McKechnie, *Magna Carta,* p. 129.

21 Max Rheinstein, ed., *Max Weber on Law in Economy and Society* (Cambridge, Mass., 1954), p. 289.

22 James Bryce, *The American Commonwealth* (2d ed.; London and New York, 1889), I, 422-23.

23 Samuel E. Thorne, "Dr. Bonham's Case," *Law Quarterly Review,* LIV (1938), 543; Theodore T. F. Plucknett, "Bonham's Case and Judicial Review," *Harvard Law Review,* XL (1926), 30.

24 Benjamin F. Wright, *The Growth of American Constitutional Law* (New York, 1942), p. 11.

25 4 Wheaton 235, 244 (1819).

26 *Cherokee Nation v. Georgia,* 5 Peters 1, 30 (1831). This, incidentally, is one of the cases that gave rise to President Jackson's purported statement: "Marshall has made his decision, now let him enforce it." See Charles Warren, *The Supreme Court in United States History* (Boston, 1937), I, 76.

27 *Dartmouth College v. Woodward,* 4 Wheaton 520 (1819).

28 *Idem* at 581-82.

29 18 Howard 272 (1855).

30 George Ticknor Curtis, ed., *The Life and Writings of Benjamin Robbins Curtis* (Boston, 1879), II, 43.

31 *Idem,* p. 64.

32 *Idem,* p. 195.

33 18 Howard at 276-77.

34 Charles G. Haines and Foster Sherwood, *The Role of the Supreme Court in American Government and Politics, 1835-1864* (Berkeley, Cal., 1957), p. 336.

35 96 U.S. 97 (1877).

36 *Idem* at 101-2.

37 *Idem* at 102.

38 Charles H. McIlwain, *The High Court of Parliament and Its Supremacy* (New Haven, Conn., 1910), p. 42.

39 For a recent example, see Sheldon Tefft, "United States v. Barnett: '"Twas a Famous Victory,'" in *Supreme Court Review* (Chicago, 1964), p. 123.

40 96 U.S. at 102.

41 *Idem* at 103-4.

42 *Idem* at 105.

43 *Idem* at 107-8.

44 110 U.S. 516 (1910).

45 *Idem* at 528-29.

46 211 U.S. 78 (1908).

47 *Idem* at 106.

48 *Malloy v. Hogan,* 378 U.S. 1 (1964).

49 302 U.S. 319, 325 (1937).

50 19 Howard 272, 277 (1857).

51 See Robert G. McCloskey, "Economic Due Process and the Supreme Court: An Exhumation and Reburial," in *Supreme Court Review* (Chicago, 1962), p. 34.

52 Learned Hand, *The Bill of Rights* (Cambridge, Mass., 1958), p. 34.

53 314 U.S. 252, 282 (1941).

54 372 U.S. 144, 186 (1963).

55 But see Judith N. Shklar, *Legalism* (Cambridge, Mass., 1964).

Magna Carta & Constitutionalism in the Commonwealth

Sir Ivor Jennings

The Great Charter which was extended to the greater part of the Commonwealth as part of the common law was that sealed by King Henry III in 1225. Indeed, it was that Charter which received the name Magna Carta. So far as I know, the name was first used in King Henry's Confirmatory Charter of 1237.[1] It first appeared on the statute book in chapter 5 of the Statute of Marlborough, 1267. The full title, *Magna Carta de libertatibus Angliae,* was used in the *inspeximus* of 1297. This *inspeximus* is the authoritative text, for it was enrolled on the Statute Roll. It was the text used by the printers of the sixteenth century and by Coke in his *Second Institutes*. Since the text was that of 1225, Magna Carta usually appeared in the printed collections of statutes as the statute of 9 Henry III. It was in this form that the territories overseas knew it, either from Coke or from the

Statutes at Large. In the *Statutes of the Realm,* however, the Record Commissioners printed the whole *inspeximus,* and so Magna Carta appeared as the statute 25 Edward I. The example was followed by the Statute Law Revision Commissioners. What is left of Magna Carta in the law of England and Wales—so far as I know it was never extended to Scotland [2]—appears as the statute 25 Edward I on page 31 of the first volume of the third edition of *Statutes Revised,* published in 1950.

Even in the seventeenth century there was confusion between King John's Charter of 1215 and King Henry's Charter of 1225. The text then in use, and indeed the only text known to exist, was that of 1225. The lawyers of the seventeenth century thought, however, that the text used by them was that of 1215. John Selden pointed out that the text in Matthew Paris contained two chapters which were not in the printed version, and we now know that they were taken from King John's Charter of 1215. They were the provisions relating to scutages and aids, in the modern connotation chapters 12 and 14. Generally speaking, however, in the great constitutional disputes of the seventeenth century the lawyers quoted from the Magna Carta of 1225 as if it were King John's Charter of 1215, to which the name Magna Carta thus became attached. Blackstone in 1759 sorted out the various charters and published the texts. Following the long historical tradition and not the statute book, he printed the Charter of 1215 as *Magna Carta regis Johannis,* and following the statute book he printed the Charter of 1225 as *Magna Carta Regis Henrici III, 9 Hen.3.* The Record Commissioners, in their volume of *Charters of Liberties,* followed this example, though in the *Statutes of the Realm* they printed *Magna Carta de libertatibus Angliae* as 25 Edward I. Even though he knows that it derives from a mistake by the chroniclers of St. Albans, no lawyer can object to the long historical tradition which gives the name Magna Carta to King

John's Charter; but he must insist that the Magna Carta available for export was that of 1225. My references will be to the latter.

The reception of English law in territories which are or have been under English or British rule and jurisdiction came about in three ways. When Englishmen settled in territories in which there was no settled system of law, they carried with them the laws and liberties of England, insofar as these were compatible with conditions in their new country. They did not, for instance, have a church established by law, nor did they take the feudal land law of England, though the land was deemed to be vested in the Crown. In conquered or ceded territories with a settled law, however, that law was presumed to continue until it was changed by or under the authority of the Crown. To this rule there were exceptions, though I need not mention them all.

First, the ceded or conquered colony came under the rule and jurisdiction of the Crown. The whole of English constitutional law therefore applied, and in particular the Crown established courts on the English model.

Second, there is authority for saying that where the existing law was contradictory to the fundamental principles of the common law, it was void. This was actually applied only to torture, which Coke regarded as inconsistent with chapter 29 of Magna Carta, but which was authorized by the Spanish law taken over by the British after the French wars.[3] This doctrine would probably have extended to imprisonment without trial, and perhaps to the whole concept of due process of law read into chapter 29.[4]

Third, there were existing laws which, by reason of their nature, could not be extended to English settlers or to the transactions—such as those covered by the whole body of commercial law—which they engendered. The tribal laws of West Africa continued to apply to members of the tribes and to the lands they occupied. Such laws could not apply to the European settlers or to

the freed slaves of Sierra Leone—though the problem of Sierra
Leone was met by regarding it as a settled colony to which English law applied. Again, the Hindu law and the Mohammedan
law of the Indian subcontinent could not apply to Christians,
whether English or Indian. These laws in fact became personal
laws governing family relationships and the ownership and devo-
lution of property.

I ought to add that many territories which were subject to British rule and jurisdiction were not, initially, classed as colonies.
They were protected states, protectorates, or mandated territories
of the League of Nations. They included most of the territories in
Africa, but not the four West African colonies, each of which had
a protectorate in the hinterland; nor the South African colonies
and Basutoland; nor Mauritius and the Seychelles, which were
regulated by the Napoleonic Codes. They also included the whole
of Malaysia and Brunei, except the Straits Settlements of Malacca,
Penang, and Singapore. The Straits Settlements were regarded as
settled colonies to which English law applied, though the settlers
were mostly Chinese.

I need not enter upon the enormous complications these rules
produced. It would be necessary to study each territory in turn in
order to show the evolution of its present legal system. Perhaps I
may take one example, that of Ceylon. The maritime provinces
were ceded by the Dutch and so the old law of the province of
Holland, the Roman-Dutch law, applied. But the Dutch had retained the Tamil personal laws, the Thesawalami, the Mohammedan personal law, which they had attempted to codify, and the
Singhalese system of tenure of land. These laws still apply, but
the British, by legislation, introduced the English system of courts
and civil procedure and, via India, the whole of English criminal
law and procedure. In 1815 the Kandyan provinces were ceded
by the Kandyan chiefs subject to the maintenance of Kandyan

law and the authority of the chiefs. After a rebellion in 1817, however, the authority of the chiefs was much diminished and in 1830 the Kandyan provinces were absorbed into the legal system of the maritime provinces, subject to the maintenance of Kandyan law, which in fact operated as a personal law and as a law relating to the tenure of land. Since 1830, too, there has been considerable application of English law by legislation, notably commercial law. Consequently, when I lectured on the legal systems of Ceylon—note the plural—I had to say something about English law, Roman-Dutch law, the Thesawalami (in a background of Hindu law), Mohammedan law, Kandyan law, and Singhalese tenures generally.

I have, however, mentioned only incidentally ways of extending English law other than by inheritance.

It will be seen that, in a conquered or ceded colony which had a legal system not applicable to settlers or to such matters as commercial transactions, a hiatus existed. Usually, it was filled by legislation. If it was not, courts administered according to "justice, equity, and good conscience," and in a few countries of the Commonwealth this latter procedure may still prevail. In effect, the courts are recognized to have a legislative function. They were and are staffed by English lawyers or by lawyers of local origin trained in English law. It was inevitable that they should regard English law, shorn of its technicalities, as exhibiting "justice, equity, and good conscience." This is, accordingly, the second method of receiving English law. It was not, however, as important as legislation.

In some places the whole of the local law was superseded by English law. In others particular parts of English law, or particular statutes, might be applied. I need not go into details because everywhere in what was formerly British Asia, except in Ceylon, English law applied, subject to the exceptions of Hindu and

Mohammedan law, where these were applicable, and to Malay custom. In what was formerly British Africa, too, English law applied except in the Republic of South Africa, Rhodesia, Mauritius, and the Seychelles, but subject to the exception of African tribal law.

When I say that English law applies, I usually mean the common law of England. This is not true in India and Pakistan, where the courts may have to fall back on "justice, equity, and good conscience." Generally speaking, however, the common law is English law as at the date of settlement or of the extension of English law by legislation. Sometimes the extension consists of the extension of an existing local law to a wider one. For instance, Ghana consists of the former Gold Coast colony and the former Gold Coast Protectorate. What was extended to the Protectorate was not the law of England but the law of the colony.

What I am emphasizing, however, is that not only the English common law but also the English statute law was extended, subject in each case to compatibility with local conditions. Magna Carta is regarded as a statute, and it was applied and extended by other statutes. It is of course true that these statutes have been incorporated into English common law by reason of the development of common-law remedies. The historians have demonstrated that many of the concepts that have been read into Magna Carta are not there. One cannot, for instance, find in Magna Carta the concepts of trial in open court, the independence of the judges, trial by jury, or habeas corpus. For that matter, due process of law is not there, though it is in one of the confirmations of Magna Carta, chapter 3 of 28 Edward III (1354): "No man of what estate or condition that he be, shall be put out of land or tenement, nor taken, nor imprisoned, nor disinherited, nor put to death, without being brought in answer by due process of law." What is important, however, is not what is in Magna Carta, but what is in the common law of a territory because of Magna Carta. The reaction against the Whig conception of history has gone too far. It is creating the episodic conception of history which tells us that the Governor quarreled with the Chief Justice because of incompatibility of temperament. I do not deny the importance of temperament; but if the Chief Justice objected to the Governor's use of imprisonment without trial, I am enough of a Whig to think of due process of law and chapter 29 of Magna Carta. There has been a progressive development of the liberties of England, and the liberties of England have been freely exported.

This does not mean that the whole of Magna Carta has been exported. All the provisions relating to tenure, its services and incidents, were obsolete after 1645, and in any case the law laid down in Littleton's *Tenures* was not exported. Again, most of the provisions relating to the administration of justice were rendered obsolete by the reforms of King Edward I. Some of the miscellaneous provisions related peculiarly to English conditions. What remained were a few provisions forbidding distraint except on the orders of a court, chapter 29, a provision giving priority to debts due to the Crown, and above all the general principle of government according to law. This general principle, I take it, is expressed in the term "constitutionalism."

The term "constitution" was used of the charter or other instrument of government in an American colony at least as early as 1739. Even the Crown colonies had constitutions, for they were governed under commissions issued to the governors setting out in some detail how the governors were to exercise their powers. The term, was, however, used *ex post facto*. It was not used contemporaneously, because it was inappropriate. In most Crown colonies the governor-in-council had both legislative and executive powers. Moreover, until the 1870s each governor received a new commission. Even in the twentieth century the legislation setting up constitutions was not described as such. We had Government of Ireland Acts, Government of India Acts, Ceylon (Legislative Council) Orders in Council, and so on. We have British North America Acts, but a Commonwealth of Australia (Constitution) Act. Even in 1909 we had a South Africa Act. In short, the idea of a constitution was really established when responsible government was conferred, though even then the use of the term was unusual. English lawyers have generally preferred "government according to law" or "the rule of law."

It might be thought that one could hardly refer to "government according to law" where both legislative and executive powers were vested in a governor or a governor-general acting with, or even without, the advice of a council nominated by him. Moreover, at the lower levels of administration the same officers —the collectors, the district commissioners, or the government agents—exercised both executive and judicial powers. This is, however, to confuse the doctrine of the separation of powers with the doctrine of the separation of authorities exercising powers. The governors-in-council could alter the law; but until they altered it they had to observe it. The distinction between legislative and executive action was clear, because legislative enactments had to be sent to London and might be disallowed. The administrative officers exercising both executive and judicial powers themselves separated the functions by having formal sittings in court for judicial business, and their decisions were subject to appeal to courts staffed by professional judges.

It is not my function to explain the intricacies of government according to law in the United Kingdom; but I must explain what was exported to the territories under British rule and jurisdiction overseas, and especially those in Asia and Africa.

First, we have the apparatus of the law itself, what one might call the essential concepts of the judicial administration of the civil and criminal law. These concepts have been exported to all parts of the Commonwealth and to most of the countries formerly under British rule and jurisdiction, even where the common law of the country concerned is by origin French or Spanish or Dutch. Some qualifications have to be made in places like Malta and Cyprus, where other European influences have been at work; but go where you will in the Commonwealth in Asia or Africa and you will find that the courts are the heirs of the courts in Westminster Hall, acting "fairly and freely, without favour and without fear," applying common-law remedies even when the wrongs are not common-law wrongs. One result of not having a written constitution in the United Kingdom is that, until very recently, the governments of the United Kingdom have not thought that the establishment of legislative, executive, and judicial institutions in a colony or protectorate was a single operation. The Crown appointed a governor and, usually, gave him legislative powers in council: but it did not empower him to establish courts or appoint judges. Those things were done by the Crown; and even in the last stages of colonial rule the colonial legal service was distinct from the civil services of the respective territories. All were appointed by the Secretary of State in the name of the Crown; but the civil servants were subordinate to the governor, whereas the judges were not.

Second, we have the apparatus ancillary to the administration of the law, above all the legal profession. In no other legal system is there an exact equivalent of the English bar. The medieval concept of the gild resulted in the establishment of common-law corporations of lawyers within walking distance of Westminster Hall. The Inns of Court and Chancery have coalesced into the four Inns: Lincoln's Inn, the Inner and the Middle Temple, and my own Inn, Gray's. Judges, Queen's counsel, and junior barristers sit cheek by jowl on the bench, and in hall is a collection of members from the junior student to the Master Treasurer, who presides over hall until the bench leaves and Mr. Senior takes over. These are the four pillars of the independence of bench and bar. The members of these four Inns have all the prejudices of the common law, not merely as principles of law and legal administration, but as eternal principles that ought to be maintained even if the law says otherwise. Because of a state of emergency it may be necessary for Parliament to authorize detention without trial: but it will not be forgotten in the Inns that this breach of chapter 29 of Magna Carta can be justified, if at all, only by the state of emergency. Some judges will not be ready to acquiesce unless the intention of Parliament is made abundantly plain, and so one gets famous dissenting judgments like those in *Rex v. Halliday*[5] and *Liversidge v. Anderson*,[6] which themselves become texts on the liberties of England. Nor must it be forgotten that the lawyers in the service of the Crown, the Attorney-General and the Solicitor-General, the Treasury Solicitor, the Director of Public Prosecutions, the Parliamentary Counsel to the Treasury, the legal advisers to the government departments, are all members of their Inns of Court, imbued with the same common-law prejudices or traditions as their brethren sitting on the bench or practicing within or at the bar.

I particularly draw your attention to the fact that, in the system of responsible government, legislation is drafted by Parliamentary Counsel or legal draftsmen who are professional lawyers in the service of the Crown. They receive instructions from civil servants acting on behalf of ministers, but they have a profound influence on the form of legislation and on much of its content. They are particularly valuable in protecting the liberties of the subject. The minister's object may perhaps be attained most simply by ignoring those liberties. The greatest happiness of the greatest number, or at least votes at the next election, may be attained by doing injustice to the smallest number. Those who are accustomed to defending John Smith against the Queen, or the owner of a small tenement against the Minister of Housing and Local Government, or a person of hostile origin against the Secretary of State, do not take kindly to injustice wheresoever, by whomsoever, and under whatsoever authority it be committed. Parliamentary Counsel and legal draftsmen are members of the bar, as vigilant as defending counsel to protect the liberties of England.

What is more, their efforts are supported in Parliament. This brings us to the third point, that the liberties of England arising out of Magna Carta have become part of the common stock of ideas. Chapter 29 can be translated into the language of Hoxton or Limehouse, and is so translated by people who have never read Magna Carta even in translation. Many people quote the authorized version of the Bible, or Shakespeare, without knowing it because much of the imagery has passed into ordinary speech. For over seven hundred years Magna Carta has been part of the law of England. It was confirmed at least fifty-five times. It was one of the earliest documents to be printed. It was argued over in the Stuart reigns. It has been quoted to many generations of schoolboys. The assumptions of the man in the street are not very different from those of the judge on the bench or the advocate at the bar. The assumptions are made articulate in Parliament; and I think that everybody agrees that the House of Commons is at its best when it uncovers a case of injustice. The minister, if he is wise, will ask for time to investigate. If he defends his department, the hounds will be after him as if he were a fox on the run. What is more, if legislative proposals are so framed as to be likely to lead to injustice, he has to defend his draft against a House which is traditionally the protector of liberty. There are lawyers in Parliament who may find themselves, unwittingly, supporting

Parliamentary Counsel against the civil servants: but most members can take a point as quickly as members of the bar.

How much of all this been exported? The answer is, I think, nearly all of it. There are, of course, no Inns of Court. There are, however, a bench and a bar which look and behave much as if they were in Westminster Hall. Many of them have, in fact, been called to the English bar. In most parts of the Commonwealth there are councils of legal education or law schools teaching the essential principles of Magna Carta. If an English lawyer goes into a court in Accra, or Lagos, or Dar-es-Salaam, or Lahore, or Delhi, or Colombo, or Kuala Lumpur, he finds himself very much at home. The technique of parliamentary drafting by government draftsmen is everywhere the same. Sir Erskine May's *Parliamentary Practice* is on the table of every legislature from Victoria, British Columbia, to Nairobi, and from Dar-es-Salaam to Hong Kong or Wellington, New Zealand. In every legislature are lawyers who speak the language of Magna Carta.

There are, however, qualifications. In British India, the Federation of Malaya, and elsewhere, it was occasionally thought necessary by the British administrations to provide themselves with powers outside the ordinary law. The troubles were not necessarily political. Armed dacoity led to the Bengal regulations; and the secret societies of the Straits Settlements have always been a problem. After 1916, however, political movements, especially nationalist and communist movements, used the technique of deliberate disobedience to law in order to embarrass the British administrations. Just as there is no longer a clear line between peace and war, so there is no clear line between civil war, or rebellion, and law and order. I am, of course, not concerned with the political aspect of the problem. I simply assert that the maintenance of law and order by traditional and well-tried methods becomes difficult, if not impossible, if a small minority of active politicians sets out deliberately to subvert the law, especially if that small minority has active or passive support from a larger part of the population. Chen Ping, for instance, never had more than two thousand men in the Malayan jungles. There the terrain was particularly favorable to guerilla warfare and his men had no great difficulty in getting supplies from isolated pockets of Chinese. Special powers were needed to deal with that situation, and to deal with a score of other situations in Asia and Africa, not all of them under British or other European rule. By special powers I mean powers for detention without trial, trial by military tribunals, the censorship of and the suppression of books and periodicals, curfew regulations, restrictions on public meetings, the prohibition of voluntary associations, and generally a denial of most, if not all, of the fundamental freedoms which can be found in English law.

British governments, which have to defend themselves in the House of Commons, have always been reluctant to authorize legislation conferring special powers. With the coming of independence local politicians seem to have less reluctance because they have, in many cases, suffered from the use of such powers. One cannot pass judgment without studying the circumstances of each country, and I think that nobody can talk in general terms about Ghana and Nigeria, Rhodesia and Malawi, Kenya and Tanzania, India and Pakistan. I know only that if one asks a specific question, such as, "Why suppress a periodical when one can prosecute for criminal libel or seditious conspiracy?" one gets the impression that the latter had not been thought of as a possibility. It is so much easier to stop publication without proving anything. Similarly, it is so much easier to clap the suspects in jail or banish them to remote areas than it is to prove a conspiracy. Even where there is an attempt to use the ordinary law, unconscionable methods of obtaining evidence may be used.

The second qualification is that frequently the parliamentary machine does not function as it does at Westminster. Constitution makers can provide for the establishment of governments: they have not yet learned how to provide for the establishment of Oppositions. There is indeed a tendency to regard a formed Opposition, as it was called in eighteenth-century Britain, as itself a conspiracy. Arguments, which I regard as specious, are used to justify a one-party state, as if nobody had heard of Adolf Hitler or even of Oliver Cromwell—if one may include such disparate characters in one sentence. Where legislation is carried by acclamation, there is little opportunity for stressing fundamental liberties and protecting the individual from injustice. Indeed, in some countries in Africa membership in the party and subscription to its fund are means for securing a quiet life.

The contemplation of the problems of the newly independent countries has led to a changed view of bills of rights. The combination of a common law suffused with the principles of Magna Carta and a Parliament active in the defense of the liberties of England was thought by English lawyers to provide all that Englishmen needed, especially when every village had its Hampden and every town its cohort of Pyms. Emphasis—perhaps undue emphasis—was placed on the purely declaratory character of the French Declarations of the Rights of Man. The late Professor A. V. Dicey, whose *Law of the Constitution* has expressed the prejudices of many English lawyers for eighty years, pointed out that such declarations of rights could be, and frequently were, suspended. He assumed, too, that they were extraneous to and independent of the ordinary course of the law. I have not studied enough foreign law to be sure that this is so. Probably it is not true; for one of the purposes of such a declaration of rights is to encourage legislatures to give effect to the declaration when dealing with positive law.

In any case, Dicey expressly excluded the United States. He did not say why, but I take it that he had in mind the inability of the President or the Congress to suspend the Bill of Rights, and the close correspondence between the Bill of Rights and the laws of the several states. This could be so in a Commonwealth country also, though he would be a bold man who did not provide for the suspension of constitutional guarantees in a country in which communal troubles were endemic. In the earlier constitutions of the Commonwealth, however, the prejudices of English lawyers prevailed. The constitutions of Canada, Australia, New Zealand, South Africa, and Newfoundland (before it was absorbed into Canada) contained no bills of rights, though in section 116 of the Australian Constitution there is a prohibition against legislation in relation to religion, and in placitum xxxi of section 51 the power of eminent domain is conferred only "on just terms." These are potent exceptions, for it was fear of discrimination in relation to religion and to the use of the power of expropriation that led some English lawyers to think, if not of bills of rights, at least of nondiscrimination clauses.

The problem which started this train of thought was that of Ireland. That problem had two aspects. First, there were the fears of the Protestant minority, whose views were strongly supported by the Unionist parties in Great Britain, that under Home Rule the administration would be Roman Catholic and that there would be prejudice against the Protestants. Since most of the landowners were Protestants, the fear related not only to the position and property of the Protestant churches, but also to land legislation involving compulsory acquisition without compensation or with inadequate compensation. In other words, what was wanted was not merely something along the lines of the First Amendment of the Constitution of the United States, but also the due process clause, at least insofar as it related to property. In the first Home Rule Bill (1885) limitations were made on legislative powers in respect of religion and corporations. In the second Bill (1893) there was also a complete due process clause. Dicey, who was active in politics as a Liberal Unionist, published a long disquisition on the restrictions on legislative power and objected that they were both inadequate and unenforceable.[7] In the third Bill, which became the Government of Ireland Act, 1914, there was only a modest nondiscrimination clause in matters relating to religion. It can be followed into the Government of Ireland Act, 1920, which is the present constitution of Northern Ireland, the Constitution of the Irish Free State, and the Constitution of Ceylon, where it became a general nondiscrimination clause in respect of "community," i.e. race, religion, and caste.

The second aspect of the Irish problem was that constitutional government on the lines of Magna Carta and the developed common law became impossible because of the illegal activities of a relatively small minority, with whom the mass of the population in three of the four provinces sympathized. Trial by jury, for instance, was impossible, because few Irish juries were prepared to convict an Irishman who was merely breaking British-made laws. Even magistrates could not always be trusted to enforce the laws. In any case, we have since learned from bitter experience that, unless the general population is prepared to risk reprisals by giving information to the police, a small minority can render the administration of justice and the enforcement of law and order exceedingly difficult. No British government could govern Ireland, maintain law and order, and administer justice according to law, without special powers in what were called Coercion Acts. Compared with what British people are prepared to put up with in wartime, these Acts were only mildly repressive, but legislation which concentrates on convicting the criminal necessarily restricts the liberty of the innocent and may result in injustice. The Southern Irish wanted a bill of rights for the same reason the Americans had. They had been governed by the British in a manner they regarded as oppressive. There was, however, no flamboyant Declaration of Independence, because most of the Irish politicians were prepared to accept the Articles of Agreement for a Treaty which they negotiated with the British politicians in 1921.

The Treaty, if we may so call it so for short, contained the usual nondiscrimination clause, in order to protect the Irish Protestants; but the Constitution contained a whole collection of fundamental rights, a few of them rather odd ones. This was the first bill of rights within the British Commonwealth, but its short life was undistinguished. The war against the British turned into a civil war. Armed resistance ceased in 1923, but the Irish Republican Army did not surrender its arms or dissolve its cadres. Public Safety Acts were passed which made the old Coercion Acts look almost as mild as a Dogs Act; and they were valid because the fundamental rights never became entrenched. Even the nondiscrimination clause ceased to be entrenched in 1932, when the Treaty was repealed under the Statute of Westminster, 1931.[8] In 1937 the Irish Free State was replaced by Eire, with a constitution more attuned to Mr. de Valera's philosophy.

I have dealt with the Irish experience at some length because it provided the precedent for India. Though some qualifications must be made, the liberties of England were in general transported to India and incorporated in the Codes. At least in the Presidency towns and some other places justice was administered as freely, as openly, and as equitably as in Westminster Hall. Many Indians were called to the English bar, and the Law Colleges were often the most flourishing colleges of the Indian universities. The qualifications on the liberties of subjects of the King-Emperor were due in the first place to dacoity or secret, armed gangsterdom. They were extended after the Indian National Con-

gress, under the inspiration of Mahatma Gandhi, began the civil
disobedience movement. The problem of India was therefore very
like the problem of Ireland, though on a vaster scale. In particular, there was not one minority to be protected but at least a score,
for minorities were created by religion, race, and caste. The greatest of the problems, that of the relations between the Hindus and
the Moslems, was never solved, despite the hard work put into it
both by Indians and by the British politicians and administrators
between 1927 and 1946. It resulted in the creation of Pakistan.

As the prospect of Indian self-government developed after
1917 it was inevitable that the idea of entrenched constitutional
guarantees, as a solution to some of the many problems involved,
should develop. The Simon Commission, which reported in
1930,[9] was against it; but in all probability Sir John (afterwards
Viscount) Simon was a pupil of Dicey's, and in any case his Report was stillborn. There was rather more support for the idea at
the Round-Table Conferences of 1930-32. The Government of
India Act, 1935, which resulted from long travail and was in
many respects a compromise between the views of Mahatma
Gandhi at the one extreme and Sir Winston Churchill at the
other, relied mainly on the powers of the Governor-General of
India and the Governors of the Provinces; but it contained some
nondiscrimination clauses which might be regarded as the nu-
cleus of a bill of rights. The Act came into force in 1937, but by
1940 it was plain that India must have self-government soon
after the end of the war. It was, however, equally plain that some
substitute had to be found for the special powers of the Governor-
General and the Governors. A judicious, if somewhat complicated, federal organization with a suitable distribution of powers
would help, but fundamentally the only solution was a bill of
rights. In fact, a special committee of the constituent assembly
had been set up before British rule ended.

The bill of rights in the Indian Constitution bears examination. It owes a little to that in the United States and rather less to the Universal Declaration of Human Rights. In the main, however, it is an attempt to formulate some of the principles of the common law with the necessary qualifications, and sometimes there are qualifications of the qualifications. In some lectures which I delivered in the University of Madras in March 1952[10] I was highly critical of it. It was in fact found to be unreasonably restrictive, especially in relation to modern property legislation, and it has since been amended. I think, however, that my criticisms were misconceived. It is plain from the considerable volume of case law which has developed around the bill of rights, that a body as able and as well trained in the common law as the Supreme Court of India can make use even of so complicated a bill of rights to defend the liberties of citizens. The Indian Constitution came not to destroy the common law but to fulfill it, by applying some of the eternal principles to Union and State legislation. My rather cursory study of American constitutional law had failed to demonstrate to me the proposition which is common form in this country, that the success of the American bills of rights has been due to the fact that they were, in the main, founded on the common law and that they have been interpreted by generations of judges trained in the common law in the great American law schools. The proposition applies, *mutatis mutandis,* to India, though the Indian bill of rights is of a very different type.

Another reason for changing one's mind was provided by events in the neighboring Ceylon. There, all that seemed necessary when the first drafts were made in 1943 was a fairly broad nondiscrimination clause. For some reason I have never been able to understand, the Ceylon Tamils, who have undoubtedly been discriminated against in respect of their language, have not used that clause. They seem to think that some enforcement clause is needed. Any American lawyer could tell them that is not so, though it was perhaps necessary in India. It is probable, however, that action would have been taken if there had been a full bill of rights with an enforcement clause. It is probable, too, that some of the other pieces of legislation passed since 1956 would have been invalidated.

The bill of rights in Pakistan's 1956 Constitution was based on that of India, though an attempt was made to produce a less complicated text. No bill of rights could, however, have prevented a military *coup d'état*. The Malayan bill of rights was similarly based on that of India. A new factor had, however, entered in 1953. The United Kingdom had become a party to the European Convention of Human Rights and extended it to all the territories for whose international relations it was responsible. These territories included a number of countries which have since become independent. When a bill of rights was thought necessary, the Colonial Office draftsmen tended to use the European Convention, adapted to suit the language and the spirit of the common law, as the basis of their drafts.

It seems probable, however, that bills of rights will be less successful in Africa than in Asia. The politicians and the peoples of the African countries of the Commonwealth are politically much less mature than those of Asia. There are few African lawyers of long and wide experience. Independence perhaps came too slowly in Asia, but the slow development of political institutions made it possible to hope—and in India the hope has so far been fulfilled—that democratic institutions and constitutional government would be maintained. In Africa, particularly in East and Central Africa, the development began from a much more backward state and it had to proceed very rapidly if Britain was not to repeat in Africa the experience it had suffered in British India in the 1940s. Constitutional government under a bill of rights implies that the rights must be firmly entrenched. The founding fathers in the African countries became so dominant through their success in obtaining independence that they find constitutional amendment almost as easy as the enactment of a Dogs Act. Nor do they find constitutional government to be easy, except by making unconstitutional government formally constitutional by constitutional amendment. As recent events in Ghana have shown, even the independence of judges is in danger. The numerous African lawyers we in the Inns of Court are privileged to call to the English bar no doubt return to their countries with the fundamental principles of Magna Carta and the common law in their minds. They have yet to demonstrate that they can be as tough as old Coke or that they are likely to be successful if they are. Even in England the parliament-men of the 1620s had to fight in a civil war in the 1640s. We owe the survival of Magna Carta and the principles of civil liberty to the Long Parliament, for even the Cavalier Parliament of Charles II could not repeal all the laws assented to by Charles I.

In one respect, probably, the British governments which secured the enactment of the independence legislation were at fault. So long as territories were colonies or protectorates, their final court of appeal was the Judicial Committee of the Privy Council which sits in Whitehall. Its handling of cases involving federal constitutions has been criticized in Canada, but its handling of cases involving civil liberty has been admirable. In the ten years from 1954 to 1963 it dealt with a dozen such cases of outstanding importance. Moreover, the fact that it invariably granted leave to appeal in any case in which a serious miscarriage of justice was alleged gave great strength to the supreme courts of the colonies. It could have been of very great assistance to a newly independent country, especially one with a new bill of rights. Independence of course implies a right to abolish appeals to the Queen in Council, and the power is conferred by the Statute of Westminster or the Independence Acts.[11] The decision of the Canadian Parliament to abolish appeals is readily understood; perhaps it was unnecessary to retain appeals from India and Pakistan; in some other cases it seems unfortunate that they were not retained.

There were and are two difficulties. The one is purely technical. The Judicial Committee advises the Queen and the decision is put into operation by Order in Council. The view that independence by itself revoked the authority of the Queen in Council has been rejected by the Judicial Committee itself.[12] The procedure is, however, possible only where the Queen's writ runs. The establishment of a republic necessarily breaks the connection with the monarchy. This difficulty could easily be overcome by legislation. Indeed, it has been overcome in the case of Malaysia, which is not a republic but which has replaced the Queen by a ruler called the Yang di-Pertuan Agong. In accordance with section 3 of the Federation of Malaya Independence Act, 1957, the Judicial Committee advises not the Queen but the Yang di-Pertuan Agong, who makes the necessary order. It would be quite easy to generalize this provision, but it has not been done.

The other difficulty is that the Judicial Committee sits in Whitehall and nearly all its active members are Lords of Appeal who also sit in the House of Lords. To appeal, therefore, involves expense. Also, the members of the Judicial Committee are unfamiliar with the conditions and even with the laws of the countries from which the appeals come to them. This difficulty could in large measure be overcome either by increasing the number of Lords of Appeal or by swearing additional members of the Privy Council who would be ready to travel by air to the capital city of the country concerned and to sit there for so long as the hearing of appeals required. Such a proposal was made by the Malayan Constitutional Commission in 1956, but it was not accepted by Her Majesty's Government. This decision was, I believe, a serious mistake. Dicey long ago pointed out that laws are enforced not by judicial authorities but by executive authorities, and that appeals to the Privy Council would not protect the Protestant minority in Ireland if the executive authorities refused to enforce Orders in Council.[13] This would be equally true in an independent country of the Commonwealth. Indeed, when the Privy Council decided, in a recent Nigerian case, against the government of the Western Region, the Constitution was forthwith amended.[14] Nevertheless, since the jurisdiction could always be removed, in most cases by ordinary legislation and in other cases by constitutional amendment, its retention would show confidence in the Judicial Committee. Besides, no court objects to being overruled by legislation or constitutional amendment.

One advantage of having a Judicial Committee sitting locally would be that fewer English counsel and more local counsel would be employed. To appear before a board of English and Scottish judges is an education in itself; and many of the barristers so employed would themselves become judges very soon. It is essential to have good judges even when they have to administer bad laws; and too many laws in some of the independent countries conflict with chapter 29 of Magna Carta. Since the bills of rights, even those taken from the European Convention for the Protection of Human Rights and Fundamental Freedoms, derive from the common law, their interpretation should be in the hands of persons skilled in the common law. The Lords of Appeal in Ordinary are the ablest of both our common lawyers and our civil lawyers, for the law of Scotland is founded on that of Rome. It would be necessary to retain in London enough Lords of Appeal to do the judicial business of the House of Lords, but a small addition to the number of Lords of Appeal, or, alternatively, the addition of more members to the Judicial Committee, would enable Her Majesty's Government to offer to the other countries of the Commonwealth the services of some of the ablest judges of the United Kingdom. I think the decision of 1956 was a mistake and should be reversed.

This is, however, a matter of machinery. My argument is that Magna Carta was taken to the Commonwealth as part of the common law. Not much work has been done on the common law which was exported. In many cases there are no early law reports. We do not know how and when the law libraries were built up. Even in old established jurisdictions there are gaps. In Ceylon in 1942, when we expected a Japanese invasion, the law officers based their view of martial law on my lecture notes, because there was no set of *Irish Reports* in the Island. Some years later, learned counsel found that there was only one set of *State Trials* in the Island. It belonged to me, and so there may not be a set there now. In Pakistan in 1954 we found that, even in Lahore, which had had a High Court in undivided India, there was a shortage of the more recondite material. These shortages were in highly developed jurisdictions. It is easy to imagine how little material there was elsewhere. I would guess—and it is a guess—that much of the law came from Blackstone's *Commentaries*.

Blackstone had in volume 4 a very fair summary of Magna Carta.[15] I think, however, that the summary was less important than the general tone of Blackstone's comments on the laws of England, which had to be administered by English judges in remote corners of a far-flung empire. Let me give you only one quotation:

> Laws, when prudently framed, are by no means subversive but rather introductive of liberty; for (as Mr. Locke has well observed) where there is no law there is no freedom. But then,

on the other hand, that constitution or frame of government, that system of laws, is alone calculated to maintain civil liberty, which leaves the subject entire master of his own conduct, except in those points wherein the public good requires some direction or restraint.[16]

In the fourteenth and subsequent editions, published in and after 1803, this passage was followed by a long footnote written by my learned predecessor, Edward Christian, the first Downing Professor of the Laws of England at Cambridge. Its material is not of high quality, but it contains one passage relevant to my theme. Christian expresses the hope that those who acquire the most intimate acquaintance with the laws and constitution of England "will always be the most convinced, that to be free, is to live in a country where the laws are just, expedient, and impartially administered, and where the subjects have perfect security that they will ever continue so; and, allowing for some slight and perhaps inevitable imperfections, that to be free, is to be born and to live under the English constitution." Christian displays his learning by quoting Cicero: *"Hanc retinete, quaeso, Quirites, quam vobis tanquam hereditatem, majores vestri reliquerunt."*

I quote these passages not to express approval of the nationalism implicit in them. I quote them only to show that English lawyers and British administrators, with all their faults, did try to pass on to those whom they advised and, for a time, ruled, the noble inheritance of liberty according to law. I have never met a lawyer in any part of the Commonwealth who did not think it his duty to hold fast to that inheritance. Magna Carta, at the latest count, belonged to twenty-three states members of the United Nations. We should, I think, encourage them to maintain its principles.

NOTES

1 *Statutes of the Realm:* Charters of Liberties, p. 28.

2 The "Magna Carta" of 1216 was extended to Ireland.

3 *Fabrigas v. Mostyn* (1774) 20 St. Tr. 81, 187; *R. v. Picton* (1812) 30 St. Tr. 225.

4 *Fabrigas v. Mostyn, loc. cit.*

5 [1917] A.C. 260.

6 [1942] A.C. 206.

7 Albert Venn Dicey, *A Leap in the Dark* (London, 1893), pp. 84-116.

8 The repeal was held to be valid in *Moore v. Attorney-General for the Irish Free State* [1935] A.C. 484.

9 Report of the Indian Statutory Commission (Cmd. 3568 and 3569).

10 Sir Ivor Jennings, *Some Characteristics of the Indian Constitution* (Madras, 1953).

11 *British Coal Corporation v. The King* [1935] A.C. 500.

12 *Ibralebbe v. The Queen* [1964] A.C. 900, a case from Ceylon.

13 Dicey, *op. cit.,* pp. 94-102.

14 *Adegbenro v. Akintola* [1963] A.C. 614.

15 William Blackstone, *Commentaries on the Laws of England* (Oxford, 1803), IV, 423-24.

16 *Idem,* I, 126.

APPENDIX

The Articles of the Barons*

[The document contains the terms on which peace was agreed between the king and the baronial representatives, probably on June 9 and 10, 1215. It was then sealed with John's great seal. It was probably this document that was solemnly accepted as a draft settlement by all the parties assembled at Runnymede on the fifteenth. Magna Carta as we now have it was drawn up in a number of copies before the conference ended on the twenty-fourth of June.]

[1] After the death of their ancestors heirs of full age shall have their inheritance on payment of the ancient relief, to be set out in the charter.

* A review of the literature on the *Articuli Baronum* is given in J. C. Holt, "The Making of Magna Carta," *English Historical Review*, LXXII (1957), 401.

[2] Heirs who are under age and who have been in wardship shall have their inheritance without relief and fine when they come of age.

[3] The guardian of the land of an heir shall take reasonable issues, customs, and services without destruction and waste of men and their goods, and if the guardian of the land has made destruction or waste, he shall lose the wardship; and the guardian shall keep up the houses, parks, fishponds, stanks, mills, and other appurtenances of the land out of the issues of the same land; and heirs shall be married without disparagement and with the advice of their nearer kinsmen.

[4] A widow shall not give anything for her dower or for her marriage portion after the death of her husband, but may remain in her house for forty days after his death and within this time her dower shall be assigned to her. Let her have her maritagium and inheritance at once.

[5] The king or bailiff shall not seize any land for debt so long as the chattels of the debtor are sufficient; nor shall the sureties of the debtor be distrained so long as the principal debtor is able to satisfy the debt; if the principal debtor shall fail to pay, if the sureties so desire let them have the lands of the debtor until the debt is fully paid, unless the principal debtor can show proof that he is discharged thereof as against the sureties.

[6] The king will not grant to any baron a license to take an aid from his own free tenants, except to ransom his body, to make his eldest son a knight, and to marry his eldest daughter once, and there shall be levied for this a reasonable aid.

[7] No one shall perform a greater service for a knight's fee than is due therefrom.

[8] Common pleas shall not follow the lord king's court, but

shall be assigned to some fixed place, and recognitions shall be taken in the counties in which they arise in this way: the king shall send two justiciars four times a year, who, with four knights of the same county chosen by the county, shall take assizes of novel disseisin, of mort d'ancestor and of darrein presentment, nor shall anyone be summoned for this except the jurors and the two parties.

[9] A freeman shall be amerced for a slight offense in accordance with the magnitude of the offense, saving his contenement; and a villein shall be amerced in the same way, saving his wainage; and a merchant in the same way, saving his merchandise, by the oath of honest men of the neighborhood.

[10] A clerk shall be amerced in respect of his lay-holding after the manner of the others aforesaid, and not in respect of his ecclesiastical benefice.

[11] No village shall be amerced for the building of bridges at river banks, unless they were anciently accustomed to do so.

[12] The measures of wine, corn, and the widths of cloth and other things shall be amended; and also weights.

[13] The assizes of novel disseisin and mort d'ancestor shall be shortened; and other assizes similarly.

[14] No sheriff shall interfere with pleas of the crown without the coroners being present; and counties and hundreds shall be at the old rents without any additional payment, except the king's demesne manors.

[15] If anyone holding of the king shall die, it shall be lawful for the sheriff or other bailiffs of the king to seize and catalogue his chattels by the view of law-worthy men, so that nothing be thence removed, until it is fully known whether any evident

debt is owed to the lord king, and then the king's debt shall be paid: the residue shall be left to the executors to fulfill the will of the deceased; and if nothing is owed to the king all the chattels shall go to the deceased.

[16] If any freeman shall die intestate, his goods shall be distributed by the hands of his nearer kinsfolk and friends and under the supervision of the Church.

[17] Widows shall not be compelled to marry so long as they prefer to live without husbands, provided always that they give security not to marry without the king's consent, if they hold of the king, or of the lords of whom they hold.

[18] No constable or other bailiff shall take corn or other chattels without immediately tendering money, unless he can have postponement by permission of the seller.

[19] No constable can compel any knight to give money in lieu of castle-guard, if he is willing to perform it in own person or by another responsible man, if he himself cannot do it for some proper reason; and if the king leads him on military service, he shall be relieved from guard in proportion to the time.

[20] No sheriff or bailiff of the king, or any other person, shall take the horses or carts of any freeman for transport duty against his will.

[21] Neither the king nor his bailiff shall take another's wood for his castles or for any other work, except with the consent of the owner of that wood.

[22] The king shall not retain the land of those who have been convicted of felony for longer than a year and a day, and the land shall thereafter be handed over to the lord of the fief.

[23] All fishweirs shall henceforth be removed altogether

from the Thames and the Medway and throughout all England.

[24] The writ which is called *Praecipe* shall henceforth not be issued to anyone regarding any tenement whereby a freeman may lose his court.

[25] If anyone has been disseised of his lands, liberties, or right, or exiled by the king, without judgment, let them at once be restored to him; and if a dispute arise over this, let it be decided by the judgment of the twenty-five barons, and those who were dispossessed by the father or the brother of the king shall have justice without delay by the judgment of their peers in the king's court, and if the king is to have the usual term of other crusaders then the archbishop and bishops shall make a decision on a fixed day from which there can be no appeal.

[26] Nothing shall be given for a writ of inquisition of life or limbs, but it shall be granted freely without fee and not denied.

[27] If anyone holds of the king by fee-farm, by socage, or by burgage, and holds of another by knight's service, the lord king shall not have the wardship of the knight's fee of the other's fief by reason of the burgage, socage, or fee-farm; nor ought he to have the wardship of the burgage, socage, or fee-farm; and a freeman shall not lose his knight's fee by reason of small serjeanties, as of those who hold any tenement by rendering for it knives or arrows or the like.

[28] No bailiff shall be able to put anyone to his law upon his own unsupported complaint without credible witnesses.

[29] The body of a freeman shall not be taken or imprisoned nor disseised nor outlawed nor exiled nor in any way destroyed, nor shall the king go upon him nor send upon him by force except by the judgment of his peers and the law of the land.

[30] Justice is to be neither delayed nor sold, nor denied.

[31] Merchants shall have safe exit and entry for buying and selling, quit from all evil tolls, by the ancient and right customs.

[32] No scutage or aid shall be imposed in the kingdom, except by common council of the realm, unless it be for ransoming the person of the king, making his eldest son a knight, and for marrying his eldest daughter once, and for this there shall be levied a reasonable aid. And let the same be done as to tallages and aids from the city of London and from other cities who have liberties and that the city of London shall have its ancient liberties in full and its free customs, as well by water as by land.

[33] It shall be lawful for anyone to leave the realm and return, reserving always the allegiance due to the king, except for a short period during time of war on grounds of public policy.

[34] If anyone who has borrowed from the Jews any sum, great or small, die before that loan be repaid, the debt shall not bear interest while his heir is under age, no matter of whom he may hold; and if the debt fall into the hands of the king, the king shall not take anything except the principal sum contained in the bond.

[35] If anyone die indebted to the Jews, his wife shall have her dower, and if any children are left, necessaries shall be provided them in keeping with the holding; and out of the residue the debt shall be paid, reserving however service due to feudal lords; and so as to debts due to others; and that guardians of the land shall return to the heir, when he comes of age, his land stocked with plough-teams and wainage according as he may reasonably support them out of the issues of the land.

[36] If anyone holding of some escheat, such as the honor of Wallingford, Nottingham, Boulogne, Lancaster, or of other escheats, which are in the hands of the king and are baronies, shall

die, his heir shall give no other relief and shall perform no other service to the king than he would have done to the baron, and the king shall hold it in the same manner in which the baron held it.

[37] All fines made wrongfully and against the law of the land for dowers, marriage portions, inheritances, and amercements shall be entirely remitted, or let it be done by judgment of the twenty-five barons, or the majority of the same, together with the archbishop and such others as he may wish to call for this purpose, so that if one or some of the twenty-five are in a similar suit they shall be removed and others substituted in their places by the rest of the twenty-five.

[38] Hostages and charters delivered to the king as sureties shall be restored.

[39] That those who dwell without the forest need not henceforth come before the justices of the forest upon a general summons, except those who are impleaded or who have become sureties; that all evil customs connected with forests, foresters, warrens and sheriffs, and river banks shall be amended by twelve knights of the county concerned, who shall be chosen by the honest men of the same county.

[40] The king shall entirely remove from their bailiwicks the relations and the whole brood of Gerard of Athée, so that they shall have no bailiwick in future, namely, Engelard, Andrew, Peter and Guy of Chanceaux, Guy of Cigogné, Matthew of Martigny and his brothers; and Godfrey his nephew and Philip Mark.

[41] That the king shall remove foreign knights, mercenaries, crossbowmen, and soldiers and serjeants who have come with horses and arms to the kingdom's hurt.

[42] That the king shall appoint as justices, constables, sheriffs, and bailiffs only such as know the law of the land and mean to observe it well.

[43] Barons who have founded abbeys, concerning which they hold charters from kings, or of which they have long-continued possession, shall have the wardship of them when vacant.

[44] If the king has disseised or removed Welshmen from lands or liberties or other things in England or Wales, they shall be immediately restored to them without plea; and if they were disseised or removed from tenements in England by the father or brother of the king without the judgment of their peers, the king shall grant them justice without delay, so that he do justice to them with respect to their English tenements according to the law of England, and their tenements in Wales according to the law of Wales, and their tenements in the marches according to the law of the march; the Welsh shall do the same to the king and his.

[45] That the king shall give up the son of Llywelyn and all hostages from Wales besides, and the charters delivered to him as security for the peace,

[46] That the king shall do towards the king of the Scots concerning the return of hostages, and concerning his franchises and his right in the same manner as he shall do to his barons in England,

unless it ought to be otherwise according to the charters which the king holds, by the judgment of the archbishop and the others he may wish to call to him.

[47] And all forests which have been made during the king's

time shall be disafforested, and a similar course shall be followed with regard to river banks that are enclosed by the king.

[48] Moreover all those customs and liberties, the observance of which the king has granted in the kingdom, as far as pertains to him and his men, shall be observed by all of the kingdom, clerks as well as laymen, as far as pertains to them and their men.

[49] This is the form of security for the observance of the peace and liberties between the king and the realm. The barons will choose twenty-five barons of the kingdom, whomsoever they will, who shall be bound with all their might to observe and hold and cause to be observed the peace and liberties which the lord king has granted them and has confirmed by his charter, so that if the king or the justiciar, or the king's bailiffs, or any of his officers shall in anything be at fault towards anyone, or shall have broken any one of the articles of the peace or of this security, and the offense be notified to four barons of the aforesaid twenty-five barons, the four said barons shall repair to the lord king, or to his justiciar if the king is out of the realm, and, laying the transgression before him, petition to have that transgression redressed without delay; and if the king, or his justiciar, shall not have redressed it, the king being out of the kingdom, within a reasonable time to be set out in the charter, the aforesaid four shall refer the matter to the rest of the twenty-five barons, and those twenty-five shall, together with the community of the whole land, distrain and distress the king in all possible ways, namely by seizing his castles, lands, possessions, and in any other way they can, until redress has been obtained as they deem fit, saving harmless the person of the king, the queen, and their children; and when redress has been obtained they shall resume their old relations towards the king. And whoever in the country desires it shall swear

to obey the orders of the said twenty-five barons and to molest the king to the utmost of his power; and the king publicly and freely shall give leave to everyone who wishes to swear and shall never forbid anyone to swear. All those moreover in the land, who of themselves and of their own accord are unwilling to swear to the twenty-five to help them in constraining and molesting the king, the king shall compel them to swear to the effect aforesaid. If any one of the twenty-five barons shall have died or departed from the land, or be incapacitated in any other manner which would prevent the aforesaid provisions from being carried out, those of the twenty-five who are left shall choose another in his place, according to their own judgment, and he shall be sworn in the same way as the others. Further, in all matters, the execution of which is entrusted to these twenty-five barons, if perchance these twenty-five are present and disagree about anything, or if some of them, after being summoned, are unwilling or unable to be present, that which the majority of those present ordain or command shall be held as fixed and established, exactly as if the whole twenty-five had concurred in this; and the said twenty-five shall swear that they will faithfully observe all that is aforesaid, and cause it to be observed with all their might. Further, the king will guarantee them by charters of the archbishop, of the bishops, and of Master Pandulf, that he will procure nothing from the lord Pope whereby any of these agreements might be revoked or diminished, and if any such thing shall be procured, it is to be considered void and null and shall never be used by him.

𝕸𝖆𝖌𝖓𝖆 𝕮𝖆𝖗𝖙𝖆

PREAMBLE

❡ Johannes Dei gratia rex Anglie, dominus Hibernie, dux Normannie et Aquitannie, et comes Andegavie, archiepiscopis, episcopis, abbatibus, comitibus, baronibus, justiciariis, forestariis, vicecomitibus, prepositis, ministris et omnibus ballivis et fidelibus suis salutem. Sciatis nos intuitu Dei et pro salute anime nostre et omnium antecessorum et heredum nostrorum, ad honorem Dei et exaltationem sancte Ecclesie, et emendacionem regni nostri, per consilium venerabilium patrum nostrorum, Stephani Cantuariensis archiepiscopi tocius Anglie primatis et sancte Romane ecclesie cardinalis, Henrici Dublinensis archiepiscopi, Willelmi Londoniensis, Petri Wintoniensis, Joscelini Bathoniensis et Glastoniensis, Hugonis Lincolniensis, Walteri Wygorniensis, Willelmi Conventriensis, et Benedicti Roffensis episcoporum; magistri Pandulfi domini pape subdiaconi et familiaris, fratris Aymerici magistri milicie Templi in Anglia; et nobilium virorum Willelmi Mariscalli comitis Penbrocie, Willelmi comitis Sarresburie, Willelmi comitis Warennie, Willelmi comitis Arundellie, Alani de Galeweya constabularii Scocie, Warini filii Geroldi, Petri filii Hereberti, Huberti de Burgo senescalli Pictavie, Hugonis de Ne-villa, Mathei filii Hereberti, Thome Basset, Alani Basset, Philippi de Albiniaco, Roberti de Roppeleia, Johannis Mariscalli, Johannis filii Hugonis et aliorum fidelium nostrorum.

John, by the grace of God, king of England, lord of Ireland, duke of Normandy and Aquitaine, and count of Anjou, to the archbishops, bishops, abbots, earls, barons, justiciars, foresters, sheriffs, stewards, servants, and to all his bailiffs and liege subjects, greeting. Know that, having regard to God and for the salvation of our souls, and those of all our ancestors and heirs, and unto the honor of God and the advancement of holy Church, and for the reform of our realm, we have granted as underwritten by advice of our venerable fathers, Stephen, archbishop of Canterbury, primate of all England and cardinal of the holy Roman Church, Henry, archbishop of Dublin, William of London, Peter of Winchester, Jocelyn of Bath and Glastonbury, Hugh of Lincoln, Walter of Worcester, William of Coventry, Benedict of Rochester, bishops; of Master Pandulf, subdeacon and member of the household of our lord the Pope, of brother Aymeric (master of the Knights of the Temple in England), and of the illustrious men William Marshal, earl of Pembroke, William, earl of Salisbury, William, earl of Warenne, William, earl of Arundel, Alan of Galloway (constable of Scotland), Waren Fitz Gerald, Peter Fitz Herbert, Hubert de Burgh (seneschal of Poitou), Hugh de Neville, Matthew Fitz Herbert, Thomas Basset, Alan Basset, Philip d'Aubigny, Robert of Roppesley, John Marshal, John Fitz Hugh, and others, our liegemen.

Appendix

CHAPTER ONE

⟨ In primis concessisse Deo et hac presenti carta nostra confirmasse, pro nobis et heredibus nostris in perpetuum, quod Anglicana ecclesia libera sit, et habeat jura sua integra, et libertates suas illesas; et ita volumus observari; quod apparet ex eo quod libertatem electionum, que maxima et magis necessaria reputatur ecclesie Anglicane, mera et spontanea volunte, ante discordiam inter nos et barones nostros motam, concessimus et carta nostra confirmavimus, et eam obtinuimus a domino papa Innocencio tercio confirmari; quam et nos observabimus et ab heredibus nostris in perpetuum bona fide volumus observari. Concessimus eciam omnibus liberis hominibus regni nostri, pro nobis et heredibus nostris in perpetuum, omnes libertates subscriptas, habendas et tenendas eis et heredibus suis, de nobis et heredibus nostris.

In the first place we have granted to God, and by this our present charter confirmed for us and our heirs forever that the English Church shall be free, and shall have her rights entire, and her liberties inviolate; and we will that it be thus observed; which is apparent from this that the freedom of elections, which is reckoned most important and very essential to the English Church, we, of our pure and unconstrained will, did grant, and did by our charter confirm and did obtain the ratification of the same from our lord, Pope Innocent III, before the quarrel arose between us and our barons: and this we will observe, and our will is that it be observed in good faith by our heirs forever. We have also granted to all freemen of our kingdom, for us and our heirs forever, all the underwritten liberties, to be had and held by them and their heirs, of us and our heirs forever.

CHAPTER TWO

⁅ Si quis comitum vel baronum nostrorum, sive aliorum tenen-
cium de nobis in capite per servicium militare, mortuus fuerit, et
cum decesserit heres suus plene etatis fuerit et relevium debeat,
habeat hereditatem suam per antiquum relevium; scilicet heres
vel heredes comitis de baronia comitis integra per centum libras;
heres vel heredes baronis de baronia integra per centum libras;
heres vel heredes militis de feodo militis integro per centum soli-
dos ad plus; et qui minus debuerit minus det secundum antiquam
consuetudinem feodorum.

*If any of our earls or barons, or others holding of us in chief by
military service shall have died, and at the time of his death his
heir shall be full of age and owe "relief," he shall have his inheritance on payment of the ancient relief, namely the heir or heirs
of an earl, £100 for a whole earl's barony; the heir or heirs of a
baron, £100 for a whole barony; the heir or heirs of a knight,
100s. at most for a whole knight's fee; and whoever owes less let
him give less, according to the ancient custom of fiefs.*

CHAPTER THREE

⁅ Si autem heres alicujus talium fuerit infra etatem et fuerit in
custodia, cum ad etatem pervenerit, habeat hereditatem suam sine
relevio et sine fine.

*If, however, the heir of any one of the aforesaid has been under
age and in wardship, let him have his inheritance without relief
and without fine when he comes of age.*

Appendix

CHAPTER FOUR

❡ Custos terre hujusmodi heredis qui infra etatem fuerit, non capiat de terra heredis nisi racionabiles exitus, et racionabiles consuetudines, et racionabilia servicia, et hoc sine destructione et vasto hominum vel rerum; et si nos commiserimus custodiam alicujus talis terre vicecomiti vel alicui alii qui de exitibus illius nobis respondere debeat, et ille destructionem de custodia fecerit vel vastum, nos ab illo capiemus emendam, et terra committatur duobus legalibus et discretis hominibus de feodo illo, qui de exitibus respondeant nobis vel ei cui eos assignaverimus; et si dederimus vel vendiderimus alicui custodiam alicujus talis terre, et ille destructionem inde fecerit vel vastum, amittat ipsam custodiam, et tradatur duobus legalibus et discretis hominibus de feodo illo quo similiter nobis respondeant sicut predictum est.

The guardian of the land of an heir who is thus under age, shall take from the land of the heir nothing but reasonable produce, reasonable customs, and reasonable services, and that without destruction or waste of men or goods; and if we have committed the wardship of the lands of any such minor to the sheriff, or to any other who is responsible to us for its issues, and he has made destruction or waste of what he holds in wardship, we will take of him amends, and the land shall be committed to two lawful and discreet men of that fee, who shall be responsible for the issues to us or to him to whom we shall assign them; and if we have given or sold the wardship of any such land to anyone and he has therein made destruction or waste, he shall lose that wardship, and it shall be transferred to two lawful and discreet men of

*that fief, who shall be responsible to us in like manner as afore-
said.*

CHAPTER FIVE

❡ Custos autem, quamdiu custodiam terre habuerit, sustentet
domos, parcos, vivaria, stagna, molendina, et cetera ad terram illam pertinencia, de exitibus terre ejusdem; et reddat heredi, cum
ad plenam etatem pervenerit, terram suam totam instauratam de
carrucis et waynagiis, secundum quod tempus waynagii exiget et
exitus terre racionabiliter poterunt sustinere.

*The guardian, moreover, so long as he has the wardship of the
land, shall keep up the houses, parks, fishponds, stanks, mills, and
other things pertaining to the land, out of the issues of the same
land; and he shall restore to the heir, when he has come to full
age, all his land, stocked with ploughs and wainage, according
as the season of husbandry shall require, and the issues of the
land can reasonably bear.*

CHAPTER SIX

❡ Heredes maritentur absque disparagacione, ita tamen quod,
antequam contrahatur matrimonium, ostendatur propinquis de
consanguinitate ipsuis heredis.

*Heirs shall be married without disparagement, yet so that be-
fore the marriage takes place the nearest in blood to that heir
shall have notice.*

CHAPTER SEVEN

 ❴ Vidua post mortem mariti sui statim et sine difficultate habeat maritagium et hereditatem suam, nec aliquid det pro dote sua, vel pro maritagio suo, vel hereditate sua quam hereditatem maritus suus et ipsa tenuerint die obitus ipsius mariti, et maneat in domo mariti sui per quadraginta dies post mortem ipsius, infra quos assignetur ei dos sua.

A widow, after the death of her husband, shall forthwith and without difficulty have her marriage portion and inheritance; nor shall she give anything for her dower, or for her marriage portion, or for the inheritance which her husband and she held on the day of the death of that husband; and she may remain in the house of her husband for forty days after his death, within which time her dower shall be assigned to her.

CHAPTER EIGHT

 ❴ Nulla vidua distringatur ad se maritandum dum voluerit vivere sine marito; ita tamen quod securitatem faciat quod se non maritabit sine assensu nostro, si de nobis tenuerit, vel sine assensu domini sui de quo tenuerit, si de alio tenuerit.

No widow shall be compelled to marry, so long as she prefers to live without a husband; provided always that she gives security not to marry without our consent, if she holds of us, or without the consent of the lord of whom she holds, if she holds of another.

CHAPTER NINE

ℂ Nec nos nec ballivi nostri seisiemus terram aliquam nec reddi-
tum pro debito aliquo, quamdiu catalla debitoris sufficiunt ad
debitum reddendum; nec plegii ipsius debitoris distringantur
quamdiu ipse capitalis debitor sufficit ad solucionem debiti; et
si capitalis debitor defecerit in solucione debiti, non habens unde
solvat, plegii respondeant de debito; et, si voluerint, habeant terras et redditus debitoris, donec sit eis satisfactum de debito quod
ante pro eo solverint, nisi capitalis debitor monstraverit se esse
quietum inde versus eosdem plegios.

*Neither we nor our bailiffs shall seize any land or rent for any
debt, so long as the chattels of the debtor are sufficient to repay
the debt; nor shall the sureties of the debtor be distrained so long
as the principal debtor is able to satisfy the debt; and if the principal debtor shall fail to pay the debt, having nothing wherewith
to pay it, then the sureties shall answer for the debt; and let them
have the lands and rents of the debtor, if they desire them, until
they are indemnified for the debt which they have paid for him,
unless the principal debtor can show proof that he is discharged
thereof as against the said sureties.*

CHAPTER TEN

ℂ Si quis mutuo ceperit aliquid a Judeis, plus vel minus, et moriatur antequam illud solvatur, debitum non usuret quamdiu
heres fuerit infra etatem, de quocumque teneat; et si debitum

illud inciderit in manus nostras, nos non capiemus nisi catallum contentum in carta.

If one who has borrowed from the Jews any sum, great or small, die before that loan be repaid, the debt shall not bear interest while the heir is under age, of whomsoever he may hold; and if the debt fall into our hands, we will not take anything except the principal sum contained in the bond.

CHAPTER ELEVEN

❨ Et si quis moriatur, et debitum debeat Judeis, uxor ejus habeat dotem suam, et nichil reddat de debito illo; et si liberi ipsius defuncti qui fuerint infra etatem remanserint, provideantur eis necessaria secundum tenementum quod fuerit defuncti, et de residuo solvatur debitum, salvo servicio dominorum; simili modo fiat de debitis qui debentur aliis quam Judeis.

And if anyone die indebted to the Jews, his wife shall have her dower and pay nothing of that debt; and if any children of the deceased are left under age, necessaries shall be provided for them in keeping with the holding of the deceased; and out of the residue the debt shall be paid, reserving, however, service due to feudal lords; in like manner let it be done touching debts due to others than Jews.

CHAPTER TWELVE

❨ Nullum scutagium vel auxilium ponatur in regno nostro, nisi per commune consilium regni nostri, nisi ad corpus nostrum redimendum, et primogenitum filium nostrum militem faciendum, et ad filiam nostram primogenitam semel maritandam, et ad hec non fiat nisi racionabile auxilium: simili modo fiat de auxiliis de civitate Londonie.

No scutage nor aid shall be imposed on our kingdom, unless by common counsel of our kingdom, except for ransoming our person, for making our eldest son a knight, and for once marrying our eldest daughter; and for these there shall not be levied more than a reasonable aid. In like manner it shall be done concerning aids from the city of London.

CHAPTER THIRTEEN

⟨[Et civitas Londonie habeat omnes antiquas libertates et liberas consuetudines suas, tam per terras, quam per aquas. Preterea volumus et concedimus quod omnes alie civitates, et burgi, et ville, et portus, habeant omnes libertates et liberas consuetudines suas.

And the city of London shall have all its ancient liberties and free customs, as well by land as by water; furthermore, we decree and grant that all other cities, boroughs, towns, and ports shall have all their liberties and free customs.

CHAPTER FOURTEEN

⟨[Et ad habendum commune consilium regni, de auxilio assidendo aliter quam in tribus casibus predictis, vel de scutagio assidendo, summoneri faciemus archiepiscopos, episcopos, abbates, comites, et majores barones, sigillatim per litteras nostras; et preterea faciemus summoneri in generali, per vicecomites et ballivos nostros, omnes illos qui de nobis tenent in capite; ad certum diem, scilicet ad terminum quadraginta dierum ad minus, et ad certum locum; et in omnibus litteris illius summonicionis causam summonicionis exprimemus; et sic facta summonicione negocium ad diem assignatum procedat secundum consilium illorum qui presentes fuerint, quamvis non omnes summoniti venerint.

And for obtaining the common counsel of the kingdom anent the assessing of an aid (except in the three cases aforesaid) or of a scutage, we will cause to be summoned the archbishops, bishops, abbots, earls, and greater barons, severally by our letters; and we will moreover cause to be summoned generally, through our sheriffs and bailiffs, all others who hold of us in chief, for a fixed date, namely, after the expiry of at least forty days, and at a fixed place; and in all letters of such summons we will specify the reason of the summons. And when the summons has thus been made, the business shall proceed on the day appointed, according to the counsel of such as are present, although not all who were summoned have come.

CHAPTER FIFTEEN

❴ Nos non concedemus de cetero alicui quod capiat auxilium de liberis hominibus suis, nisi ad corpus suum redimendum, et ad faciendum primogenitum filium suum militem, et ad primogenitam filiam suam semel maritandam, et ad hec non fiat nisi racionabile auxilium.

We will not for the future grant to anyone license to take an aid from his own free tenants, except to ransom his body, to make his eldest son a knight, and once to marry his eldest daughter;

and on each of these occasions there shall be levied only a reason-
able aid.

CHAPTER SIXTEEN

❲ Nullus distringatur ad faciendum majus servicium de feodo
militis, nec de alio libero tenemento, quam inde debetur.

No one shall be distrained for performance of greater service
for a knight's fee, or for any other free tenement, than is due
therefrom.

CHAPTER SEVENTEEN

❲ Communia placita non sequantur curiam nostram sed tenean-
tur in aliquo loco certo.

Common pleas shall not follow our court, but shall be held in
some fixed place.

CHAPTER EIGHTEEN

❲ Recogniciones de nova dissaisina, de morte antecessoris, et de
ultima presentacione, non capiantur nisi in suis comitatibus et hoc
modo; nos, vel si extra regnum fuerimus, capitalis justiciarius
noster, mittemus duos justiciarios per unumquemque comitatum
per quatuor vices in anno, qui, cum quatuor militibus cujuslibet
comitatus electis per comitatum, capiant in comitatu et in die et
loco comitatus assisas predictas.

Inquests of novel disseisin, of mort d'ancestor, and of darrein presentment shall not be held elsewhere than in their own county courts, and that in manner following,—We, or, if we should be out of the realm, our chief justiciar, will send two justiciars through every county four times a year, who shall, along with four knights of the county chosen by the county, hold the said assizes in the county court, on the day and in the place of meeting of that court.

CHAPTER NINETEEN

❨ Et si in die comitatus assise predicte capi non possint, tot milites et libere tenentes remaneant de illis qui interfuerint comitatui die illo, per quos possint judicia sufficienter fieri, secundum quod negocium fuerit majus vel minus.

And if any of the said assizes cannot be taken on the day of the county court, let there remain of the knights and freeholders, who were present at the county court on that day, as many as may be required for the efficient making of judgments, according as the business be more or less.

CHAPTER TWENTY

❨ Liber homo non amercietur pro parvo delicto, nisi secundum modum delicti; et pro magno delicto amercietur secundum magnitudinem delicti, salvo contenemento suo; et mercator eodem modo, salva mercandisa sua; et villanus eodem modo amercietur salvo waynagio suo, si inciderint in misericordiam nostram; et nulla predictarum misericordiarum ponatur, nisi per sacramentum proborum hominum de visneto.

A freeman shall not be amerced for a slight offense, except in accordance with the degree of the offense; and for a grave offense he shall be amerced in accordance with the gravity of the offense, yet saving always his "contenement"; and a merchant in the same way, saving his "merchandise"; and a villein shall be amerced in the same way, saving his "wainage"—if they have fallen into our mercy: and none of the aforesaid amercements shall be imposed except by the oath of honest men of the neighborhood.

CHAPTER TWENTY-ONE

❲ Comites et barones non amercientur nisi per pares suos, et non nisi secundum modum delicti.

Earls and barons shall not be amerced except through their peers, and only in accordance with the degree of the offense.

CHAPTER TWENTY-TWO

❲ Nullus clericus amercietur de laico tenemento suo, nisi secundum modum aliorum predictorum, et non secundum quantitatem beneficii sui ecclesiastici.

A clerk shall not be amerced in respect of his lay holding except after the manner of the others aforesaid; further, he shall not be amerced in accordance with the extent of his ecclesiastical benefice.

CHAPTER TWENTY-THREE

❲ Nec villa nec homo distringatur facere pontes ad riparias, nisi qui ab antiquo et de jure facere debent.

No village or individual shall be compelled to make bridges at river banks, except those who from of old were legally bound to do so.

CHAPTER TWENTY-FOUR

❲ Nullus vicecomes, constabularius, coronatores, vel alii ballivi nostri, teneant placita corone nostre.

No sheriff, constable, coroners, or others of our bailiffs, shall hold pleas of our Crown.

CHAPTER TWENTY-FIVE

❲ Omnes comitatus, hundrede, wapentakii, et trethingii, sint ad antiquas firmas absque ullo incremento, exceptis dominicis maneriis nostris.

All counties, hundreds, wapentakes, and trithings (except our demesne manors) shall remain at the old rents, and without any additional payment.

CHAPTER TWENTY-SIX

◖ Si aliquis tenens de nobis laicum feodum moriatur, et vicecomes vel ballivus noster ostendat litteras nostras patentes de
summonicione nostra de debito quod defunctus nobis debuit,
liceat vicecomiti vel ballivo nostro attachiare, et inbreviare catalla
defuncti, inventa in laico feodo, ad valenciam illius debiti, per
visum legalium hominum, ita tamen quod nichil inde amoveatur,
donec persolvatur nobis debitum quod clarum fuerit; et residuum
relinquatur executoribus ad faciendum testamentum defuncti; et,
si nichil nobis debeatur ab ipso, omnia catalla cedant defuncto,
salvis uxori ipsius et pueris racionabilibus partibus suis.

*If anyone holding of us a lay fief shall die, and our sheriff or
bailiff shall exhibit our letters patent of summons for a debt
which the deceased owed to us, it shall be lawful for our sheriff or
bailiff to attach and catalogue chattels of the deceased, found
upon the lay fief, to the value of that debt, at the sight of law-
worthy men, provided always that nothing whatever be thence
removed until the debt which is evident shall be fully paid to us;
and the residue shall be left to the executors to fulfill the will of
the deceased; and if there be nothing due from him to us, all the
chattels shall go to the deceased, saving to his wife and children
their reasonable shares.*

CHAPTER TWENTY-SEVEN

⟨ Si aliquis liber homo intestatus decesserit, catalla sua per manus propinquorum parentum et amicorum suorum, per visum ecclesie distribuantur, salvis unicuique debitis que defunctus ei debebat.

If any freeman shall die intestate, his chattels shall be distributed by the hands of his nearest kinsfolk and friends, under supervision of the Church, saving to every one the debts which the deceased owed to him.

CHAPTER TWENTY-EIGHT

⟨ Nullus constabularius, vel alius ballivus noster, capiat blada vel alia catalla alicujus, nisi statim inde reddat denarios, aut respectum inde habere possit de voluntate venditoris.

No constable or other bailiff of ours shall take corn or other provisions from anyone without immediately tendering money therefor, unless he can have postponement thereof by permission of the seller.

CHAPTER TWENTY-NINE

⟨ Nullus constabularius distringat aliquem militem ad dandum denarios pro custodia castri, si facere voluerit custodiam illam in propria persona sua, vel per alium probum hominem, si ipse eam

facere non possit propter racionabilem causam; et si nos duxeri-
mus vel miserimus eum in exercitum, erit quietus de custodia,
secundum quantitatem temporis quo per nos fuerit in exercitu.

No constable shall compel any knight to give money in lieu of
castle-guard, when he is willing to perform it in his own person,
or (if he himself cannot do it from any reasonable cause) then by
another responsible man. Further, if we have led or sent him
upon military service, he shall be relieved from guard in propor-
tion to the time during which he has been on service because of
us.

CHAPTER THIRTY

⟨[Nullus vicecomes, vel ballivus noster, vel aliquis alius, capiat
equos vel carectas alicujus liberi hominis pro cariagio faciendo,
nisi de voluntate ipsius liberi hominis.

No sheriff or bailiff of ours, or other person, shall take the
horses or carts of any freeman for transport duty, against the will
of the said freeman.

CHAPTER THIRTY-ONE

⟨[Nec nos nec ballivi nostri capiemus alienum boscum ad castra,
vel alia agenda nostra, nisi per voluntatem ipsius cujus boscus ille
fuerit.

Neither we nor our bailiffs shall take, for our castles or for any
other work of ours, wood which is not ours, against the will of the
owner of that wood.

CHAPTER THIRTY-TWO

◖ Nos non tenebimus terras illorum qui convicti fuerint de felonia, nisi per unum annum et unum diem, et tunc reddantur terre dominis feodorum.

We will not retain beyond one year and one day, the lands of those who have been convicted of felony, and the lands shall thereafter be handed over to the lords of the fiefs.

CHAPTER THIRTY-THREE

◖ Omnes kydelli de cetero deponantur penitus de Tamisia, et de Medewaye, et per totam Angliam, nisi per costeram maris.

All kydells for the future shall be removed altogether from Thames and Medway, and throughout all England, except upon the seashore.

CHAPTER THIRTY-FOUR

◖ Breve quod vocatur *Precipe* de cetero non fiat alicui de aliquo tenemento unde liber homo amittere possit curiam suam.

The writ which is called praecipe *shall not for the future be issued to anyone, regarding any tenement whereby a freeman may lose his court.*

129

CHAPTER THIRTY-FIVE

⟦ Una mensura vini sit per totum regnum nostrum, et una mensura cervisie, et una mensura bladi, scilicet quarterium Londonie, et una latitudo pannorum tinctorum et russetorum et halbergectorum, scilicet due ulne infra listas; de ponderibus autem sit ut de mensuris.

Let there be one measure of wine throughout our whole realm; and one measure of ale; and one measure of corn, to wit, "the London quarter"; and one width of cloth (whether dyed, or russet, or "Halberget"), to wit, two ells within the selvedges; of weights also let it be as of measures.

CHAPTER THIRTY-SIX

⟦ Nichil detur vel capiatur de cetero pro brevi inquisicionis de vita vel membris, sed gratis concedatur et non negetur.

Nothing in future shall be given or taken for a writ of inquisition of life or limbs, but freely it shall be granted, and never denied.

CHAPTER THIRTY-SEVEN

⟦ Si aliquis teneat de nobis per feodifirmam, vel per sokagium, vel per burgagium, et de alio terram teneat per servicium militare, nos non habebimus custodiam heredis nec terre sue que est de feodo alterius, occasione illius feodifirme, vel sokagii, vel burgagii; nec habebimus custodiam illius feodifirme, vel sokagii, vel burgagii, nisi ipsa feodifirma debeat servicium militare. Nos non habebimus custodiam heredis vel terre alicujus, quam tenet de alio per servicium militare, occasione alicujus parve serjanterie quam tenet de nobis per servicium reddendi nobis cultellos, vel sagittas, vel hujusmodi.

If anyone holds of us by fee-farm, by socage, or by burgage, and holds also land of another lord by knight's service, we will not (by reason of that fee-farm, socage, or burgage), have the wardship of the heir, or of such land of his as is of the fief of that other; nor shall we have wardship of that fee-farm, socage, or burgage, unless such fee-farm owes knight's service. We will not by reason of any small serjeanty which anyone may hold of us by the service of rendering to us knives, arrows, or the like, have wardship of his heir or of the land which he holds of another lord by knight's service.

CHAPTER THIRTY-EIGHT

❨ Nullus ballivus ponat de cetero aliquem ad legem simplici loquela sua, sine testibus fidelibus ad hoc inductis.

No bailiff for the future shall, upon his own unsupported complaint, put anyone to his "law," without credible witnesses brought for this purpose.

CHAPTER THIRTY-NINE

❡ Nullus liber homo capiatur vel imprisonetur, aut disseisiatur, aut utlagetur, aut exuletur, aut aliquo modo destruatur, nec super eum ibimus, nec super eum mittemus, nisi per legale judicium parium suorum vel per legem terre.

No freemen shall be taken or {and} imprisoned or disseised or exiled or in any way destroyed, nor will we go upon him nor send upon him, except by the lawful judgment of his peers or {and} by the law of the land.

CHAPTER FORTY

❡ Nulli vendemus, nulli negabimus, aut differemus, rectum aut justiciam.

To no one will we sell, to no one will we refuse or delay, right or justice.

CHAPTER FORTY-ONE

❡ Omnes mercatores habeant salvum et securum exire de Anglia, et venire in Angliam, et morari et ire per Angliam, tam per terram quam per aquam, ad emendum et vendendum, sine omnibus malis toltis, per antiquas et rectas consuetudines, preterquam in tempore gwerre, et si sint de terra contra nos gwerrina; et si tales inveniantur in terra nostra in principio gwerre, attachientur

sine dampno corporum et rerum, donec sciatur a nobis vel capitali
justiciario nostro quomodo mercatores terre nostre tractentur, qui
tunc invenientur in terra contra nos gwerrina; et si nostri salvi
sint ibi, alii salvi sint in terra nostra.

*All merchants shall have safe and secure exit from England,
and entry to England, with the right to tarry there and to move
about as well by land as by water, for buying and selling by the
ancient and right customs, quit from all evil tolls, except (in time
of war) such merchants as are of the land at war with us. And if
such are found in our land at the beginning of the war, they shall
be detained, without injury to their bodies or goods, until information be received by us, or by our chief justiciar, how the merchants of our land found in the land at war with us are treated;
and if our men are safe there, the others shall be safe in our
land.*

CHAPTER FORTY-TWO

❲ Liceat unicuique de cetero exire de regno nostro, et redire,
salvo et secure, per terram et per aquam, salva fide nostra, nisi
tempore gwerre per aliquod breve tempus, propter communem
utilitatem regni, exceptis imprisonatis et utlagatis secundum
legem regni, et gente de terra contra nos gwerrina, et mercatori-
bus de quibus fiat sicut predictum est.

*It shall be lawful in future for anyone (excepting always those
imprisoned or outlawed in accordance with the law of the kingdom, and natives of any country at war with us, and merchants,
who shall be treated as is above provided) to leave our kingdom
and to return, safe and secure by land and water, except for a*

short period in time of war, on grounds of public policy—reserving always the allegiance due to us.

CHAPTER FORTY-THREE

⟪ Si quis tenuerit de aliqua eskaeta, sicut de honore Wallingfordie, Notingeham, Bolonie, Lancastrie vel de aliis eskaetis, que sunt in manu nostra, et sunt baronie, et obierit, heres ejus non det aliud relevium, nec faciat nobis aliud servicium quam faceret baroni si baronia illa esset in manu baronis; et nos eodem modo eam tenebimus quo baro eam tenuit.

If anyone holding of some escheat (such as the honor of Wallingford, Nottingham, Boulogne, Lancaster, or of other escheats which are in our hands and are baronies) shall die, his heir shall give no other relief, and perform no other service to us than he would have done to the baron, if that barony had been in the baron's hand; and we shall hold it in the same manner in which the baron held it.

CHAPTER FORTY-FOUR

⟪ Homines qui manent extra forestam non veniant de cetero coram justiciariis nostris de foresta per communes summoniciones, nisi sint in placito, vel plegii alicujus vel aliquorum, qui attachiati sint pro foresta.

Men who dwell without the forest need not henceforth come before our justiciars of the forest upon a general summons, except

*those who are impleaded, or who have become sureties for any
person or persons attached for forest offenses.*

CHAPTER FORTY-FIVE

⟨[Nos non faciemus justiciarios, constabularios, vicecomites vel
ballivos, nisi de talibus qui sciant legem regni et eam bene velint
observare.

*We will appoint as justices, constables, sheriffs, or bailiffs only
such as know the law of the realm and mean to observe it well.*

CHAPTER FORTY-SIX

⟨[Omnes barones qui fundaverunt abbatias, unde habent cartas
regum Anglie, vel antiquam tenuram, habeant earum custodiam
cum vacaverint, sicut habere debent.

*All barons who have founded abbeys, concerning which they
hold charters from the kings of England, or of which they have
long-continued possession, shall have the wardship of them, when
vacant, as they ought to have.*

CHAPTER FORTY-SEVEN

⟨[Omnes foreste que afforestate sunt tempore nostro, statim de-
afforestentur; et ita fiat de repariis que per nos tempore nostro
posite sunt in defenso.

*All forests that have been made such in our time shall forth-
with be disafforested; and a similar course shall be followed with*

regard to river banks that have been placed "in defense" by us in our time.

CHAPTER FORTY-EIGHT

❲ Omnes male consuetudines de forestis et warennis, et de forestariis et warennariis, vicecomitibus et eorum ministris, repariis et earum custodibus, statim inquirantur in quolibet comitatu per duodecim milites juratos de eodem comitatu, qui debent eligi per probos homines ejusdem comitatus, et infra quadraginta dies post inquisicionem factam, penitus, ita quod numquam revocentur, deleantur per eosdem, ita quod nos hoc sciamus prius, vel justiciarius noster, si in Anglia non fuerimus.

All evil customs connected with forests and warrens, foresters and warreners, sheriffs and their officers, river banks and their wardens, shall immediately be inquired into in each county by twelve sworn knights of the same county chosen by the honest men of the same county, and shall, within forty days of the said inquest, be utterly abolished, so as never to be restored, provided always that we previously have intimation thereof, or our justiciar, if we should not be in England.

CHAPTER FORTY-NINE

❲ Omnes obsides et cartas statim reddemus que liberate fuerunt nobis ab Anglicis in securitatem pacis vel fidelis servicii.

We will immediately restore all hostages and charters delivered to us by Englishmen, as sureties of the peace or of faithful service.

CHAPTER FIFTY

❲ Nos amovebimus penitus de balliis parentes Gerardi de Athyes, quod de cetero nullam habeant balliam in Anglia; Engelardum de Cygony, Petrum et Gionem et Andream, de Cancellis, Gionem de Cygony, Galfridum de Martinny et fratres ejus, Philippum Marci et fratres ejus, et Galfridum nepotem ejus, et totam sequelam eorundem.

We will entirely remove from their bailiwicks, the relations of Gerard of Athée (so that in future they shall have no bailiwick in England); namely, Engelard of Cigogné, Peter, Guy, and Andrew of Chanceaux, Guy of Cigogné, Geoffrey of Martigny with his brothers, Philip Mark with his brothers and his nephew Geoffrey, and the whole brood of the same.

CHAPTER FIFTY-ONE

❲ Et statim post pacis reformacionem amovebimus de regno omnes alienigenas milites, balistarios, servientes, stipendiarios, qui venerint cum equis et armis ad nocumentum regni.

As soon as peace is restored, we will banish from the kingdom all foreign-born knights, crossbowmen, serjeants, and mercenary soldiers who have come with horses and arms to the kingdom's hurt.

CHAPTER FIFTY-TWO

❬ Si quis fuerit disseisitus vel elongatus per nos sine legali judicio parium suorum, de terris, castellis, libertatibus, vel jure suo, statim ea ei restituemus; et si contentio super hoc orta fuerit, tunc inde fiat per judicium viginti quinque baronum, de quibus fit mencio inferius in securitate pacis: de omnibus autem illis de quibus aliquis disseisitus fuerit vel elongatus sine legali judicio parium suorum, per Henricum regem patrem nostrum vel per Richardum regem fratrem nostrum, que in manu nostra habemus, vel que alii tenent que nos oporteat warantizare, respectum habebimus usque ad communem terminum crucesignatorum; exceptis illis de quibus placitum motum fuit vel inquisicio facta per preceptum nostrum, ante suscepcionem crucis nostre: cum autem redierimus de peregrinacione nostra, vel si forte remanserimus a peregrinacione nostra, statim inde plenam justiciam exhibebimus.

If anyone has been dispossessed or removed by us, without the legal judgment of his peers, from his lands, castles, franchises, or from his right, we will immediately restore them to him; and if a dispute arise over this, then let it be decided by the five-and-twenty barons of whom mention is made below in the clause for securing the peace. Moreover, for all those possessions, from which anyone has, without the lawful judgment of his peers, been disseised or removed, by our father, King Henry, or by our brother, King Richard, and which we retain in our hand (or which are possessed by others, to whom we are bound to warrant them) we shall have respite until the usual term of crusaders; excepting those things about which a plea has been raised, or an

*inquest made by our order, before our taking of the cross; but as
soon as we return from our expedition (or if perchance we desist
from the expedition) we will immediately grant full justice
therein.*

CHAPTER FIFTY-THREE

❲ Eundem autem respectum habebimus, et eodem modo de jus-
ticia exhibenda de forestis deafforestandis vel remansuris forestis,
quas Henricus pater noster vel Richardus frater noster affores-
taverunt, et de custodiis terrarum que sunt de alieno feodo,
cujusmodi custodias hucusque habuimus occasione feodi quod
aliquis de nobis tenuit per servicium militare, et de abbaciis que
fundate fuerint in feodo alterius quam nostro, in quibus dominus
feodi dixerit se jus habere; et cum redierimus, vel si remanserimus a peregrinacione nostra, super hiis conquerentibus plenam
justiciam statim exhibebimus.

*We shall have, moreover, the same respite and in the same
manner in rendering justice concerning the disafforestation or
retention of those forests which Henry our father and Richard
our brother afforested, and concerning the wardship of lands
which are of the fief of another (namely, such wardships as we
have hitherto had by reason of a fief which anyone held of us by
knight's service), and concerning abbeys founded on other fiefs
than our own, in which the lord of the fee claims to have right;
and when we have returned, or if we desist from our expedition,
we will immediately grant full justice to all who complain of
such things.*

CHAPTER FIFTY-FOUR

⁋ Nullus capiatur nec imprisonetur propter appellum femine de morte alterius quam viri sui.

No one shall be arrested or imprisoned upon the appeal of a woman, for the death of any other than her husband.

CHAPTER FIFTY-FIVE

⁋ Omnes fines qui injuste et contra legem terre facti sunt nobiscum, et omnia amerciamenta facta injuste et contra legem terre, omnino condonentur, vel fiat inde per judicium viginti quinque baronum de quibus fit mencio inferius in securitate pacis, vel per judicium majoris partis eorundem, una cum predicto Stephano Cantuariensi archiepiscopo, si interesse poterit, et aliis quos secum ad hoc vocare voluerit: et si interesse non poterit, nichilominus procedat negocium sine eo, ita quod, si aliquis vel aliqui de predictis viginti quinque baronibus fuerint in simili querela, amoveantur quantum ad hoc judicium, et alii loco eorum per residuos de eisdem viginti quinque, tantum ad hoc faciendum electi et jurati substituantur.

All fines made with us unjustly and against the law of the land, and all amercements imposed unjustly and against the law of the land, shall be entirely remitted, or else it shall be done concerning them according to the decision of the five-and-twenty barons of whom mention is made below in the clause for securing the peace, or according to the judgment of the majority of the same, along with the aforesaid Stephen, archbishop of Canterbury, if he can be present, and such others as he may wish to bring with him for this purpose, and if he cannot be present the business shall nevertheless proceed without him, provided always that if any one or more of the aforesaid five-and-twenty barons are in a similar suit, they shall be removed as far as concerns this particular judgment, others being substituted in their places after having been selected by the rest of the same five-and-twenty for this purpose only, and after having been sworn.

CHAPTER FIFTY-SIX

❡ Si nos disseisivimus vel elongavimus Walenses de terris vel libertatibus vel rebus aliis, sine legali judicio parium suorum, in Anglia vel in Wallia, eis statim reddantur; et si contencio super hoc orta fuerit, tunc inde fiat in marchia per judicium parium suorum, de tenementis Anglie secundum legem Anglie, de tenementis Wallie secundum legem Wallie, de tenementis marchie secundum legem marchie. Idem facient Walenses nobis et nostris.

If we have disseised or removed Welshmen from lands or liberties, or other things, without the legal judgment of their peers in England or in Wales, they shall be immediately restored to them; and if a dispute arise over this, then let it be decided in the marches by the judgment of their peers; for tenements in England according to the law of England, for tenements in Wales according to the law of Wales, and for tenements in the marches according to the law of the marches. Welshmen shall do the same to us and ours.

CHAPTER FIFTY-SEVEN

❡ De omnibus autem illis de quibus aliquis Walensium disseistus fuerit vel elongatus sine legali judicio parium suorum per Henricum regem patrem nostrum vel Ricardum regem fratrem nostrum, que nos in manu nostra habemus, vel que alii tenent que nos oporteat warantizare, respectum habebimus usque ad communem terminum crucesignatorum, illis exceptis de quibus placitum motum fuit vel inquisicio facta per preceptum nostrum ante suscepcionem crucis nostre: cum autem redierimus, vel si forte remanserimus a peregrinacione nostra, statim eis inde plenam justiciam exhibebimus, secundum leges Walensium et partes predictas.

Further, for all those possessions from which any Welshman has, without the lawful judgment of his peers, been disseised or removed by King Henry our father, or King Richard our brother, and which we retain in our hand (or which are possessed by others, to whom we are bound to warrant them) we shall have respite until the usual term of crusaders; excepting those things about which a plea has been raised or an inquest made by our order before we took the cross; but as soon as we return (or if perchance we desist from our expedition), we will immediately grant full justice in accordance with the laws of the Welsh and in relation to the foresaid regions.

Appendix

CHAPTER FIFTY-EIGHT

⁋ Nos reddemus filium Lewelini statim, et omnes obsides de Wallia, et cartas que nobis liberate fuerunt in securitatem pacis.

We will immediately give up the son of Llywelyn and all the hostages of Wales, and the charters delivered to us as security for the peace.

CHAPTER FIFTY-NINE

⁋ Nos faciemus Alexandro regi Scottorum de sororibus suis, et obsidibus reddendis, et libertatibus suis, et jure suo, secundum formam in qua faciemus aliis baronibus nostris Anglie, nisi aliter esse debeat per cartas quas habemus de Willelmo patre ipsius, quondam rege Scottorum; et hoc erit per judicium parium suorum in curia nostra.

We will do towards Alexander, king of Scots, concerning the return of his sisters and his hostages, and concerning his franchises, and his right, in the same manner as we shall do towards our other barons of England, unless it ought to be otherwise according to the charters which we hold from William his father, formerly king of Scots; and this shall be according to the judgment of his peers in our court.

CHAPTER SIXTY

⟨[Omnes autem istas consuetudines predictas et libertates quas nos concessimus in regno nostro tenendas quantum ad nos pertinet erga nostros, omnes de regno nostro, tam clerici quam laici, observent quantum ad se pertinet erga suos.

Moreover, all these aforesaid customs and liberties, the observance of which we have granted in our kingdom as far as pertains to us towards our men, shall be observed by all of our kingdom, as well clergy as laymen, as far as pertains to them towards their men.

CHAPTER SIXTY-ONE

⟨[Cum autem pro Deo, et ad emendacionem regni nostri, et ad melius sopiendam discordiam inter nos et barones nostros ortam, hec omnia predicta concesserimus, volentes ea integra et firma stabilitate in perpetuum guadere, facimus et concedimus eis securitatem subscriptam; videlicet quod barones eligant viginti quinque barones de regno quos voluerint, qui debeant pro totis viribus suis observare, tenere, et facere observari, pacem et libertates quas eis concessimus, et hac presenti carta nostra confirmavimus, ita scilicet quod, si nos, vel justiciarius noster, vel ballivi nostri, vel aliquis de ministris nostris, in aliquo erga aliquem deliquerimus, vel aliquem articulorum pacis aut securitatis transgressi fuerimus, et delictum ostensum fuerit quatuor baronibus de predictis viginti quinque baronibus, illi quatuor barones accedant ad nos vel ad justiciarum nostrum, si fuerimus extra regnum,

proponentes nobis excessum, petent ut excessum illum sine di-
lacione faciamus emendari. Et si nos excessum non emendaveri-
mus, vel, si fuerimus extra regnum justiciarius noster non emen-
daverit, infra tempus quadraginta dierum computandum a
tempore quo monstratum fuerit nobis vel justiciario nostro si extra regnum fuerimus, predicti quatuor barones referant causam
illam ad residuos de illis viginti quinque baronibus, et illi viginti
quinque barones cum communa tocius terre distringent et
gravabunt nos modis omnibus quibus poterunt, scilicet per
capcionem castrorum, terrarum, possessionum, et aliis modis
quibus poterunt, donec fuerit emendatum secundum arbitrium
eorum, salva persona nostra et regine nostre et liberorum nostrorum; et cum fuerit emendatum intendent nobis sicut prius
fecerunt. Et quicumque voluerit de terra juret quod ad predicta
omnia exequenda parebit mandatis predictorum viginti quinque
baronum, et quod gravabit nos pro posse suo cum ipsis, et nos
publice et libere damus licenciam jurandi cuilibet qui jurare
voluerit, et nulli umquam jurare prohibebimus. Omnes autem
illos de terra qui per se et sponte sua noluerint jurare viginti
quinque baronibus, de distringendo et gravando nos cum eis,
faciemus jurare eosdem de mandato nostro, sicut predictum est. Et
si aliquis de viginti quinque baronibus decesserit, vel a terra reces-
serit, vel aliquo alio modo impeditus fuerit, quominus ista predicta possent exequi, qui residui fuerint de predictis viginti
quinque baronibus eligant alium loco ipsius, pro arbitrio suo, qui
simili modo erit juratus quo et ceteri. In omnibus autem que istis
viginti quinque baronibus committuntur exequenda, si forte ipsi
viginti quinque presentes fuerint, et inter se super re aliqua dis-
cordaverint, vel aliqui ex eis summoniti nolint vel nequeant interesse, ratum habeatur et firmum quod major pars eorum qui
presentes fuerint providerit, vel preceperit, ac si omnes viginti
quinque in hoc consensissent; et predicti viginti quinque jurent

quod omnia antedicta fideliter observabunt, et pro toto posse suo facient observari. Et nos nichil impetrabimus ab aliquo, per nos nec per alium, per quod aliqua istarum concessionum et libertatum revocetur vel minuatur; et, si aliquid tale impetratum fuerit, irritum sit et inane et numquam eo utemur per nos nec per alium.

Since, moreover, for God and the amendment of our kingdom and for the better allaying of the quarrel that has arisen between us and our barons, we have granted all these concessions, desirous that they should enjoy them in complete and firm endurance forever, we give and grant to them the underwritten security, namely, that the barons choose five-and-twenty barons of the kingdom, whomsoever they will, who shall be bound with all their might, to observe and hold, and cause to be observed, the peace and liberties we have granted and confirmed to them by this our present Charter, so that if we, or our justiciar, or our bailiffs or any one of our officers, shall in anything be at fault towards anyone, or shall have broken any one of the articles of the peace or of this security, and the offense be notified to four barons of the foresaid five-and-twenty, the said four barons shall repair to us (or our justiciar, if we are out of the realm) and, laying the transgression before us, petition to have that transgression redressed without delay. And if we shall not have corrected the transgression (or, in the event of our being out of the realm, if our justiciar shall not have corrected it) within forty days, reckoning from the time it has been intimated to us (or to our justiciar, if we should be out of the realm), the four barons aforesaid shall refer that matter to the rest of the five-and-twenty barons, and those five-and-twenty barons shall, together with the community of the whole land, distrain and distress us in all possible ways, namely, by seizing our castles, lands, possessions, and in any other way they can, until redress has been obtained as they deem fit, saving harmless our own person, and the persons of our queen and children; and when redress has been obtained, they shall resume their old relations towards us. And let whoever in the country desires it, swear to obey the orders of the said five-and-twenty barons for the execution of all the aforesaid matters, and along with them, to molest us to the utmost of his power; and we publicly and freely grant leave to everyone who wishes to swear, and we shall never forbid anyone to swear. All those, moreover, in the land who of themselves and of their own accord are unwilling to swear to the twenty-five to help them in constraining and molesting us, we shall by our command compel the same to swear to the effect foresaid. And if any one of the five-and-twenty barons shall have died or departed from the land, or be incapacitated in any other manner which would prevent the foresaid provisions being carried out, those of the said twenty-five barons who are left shall choose another in his place according to their own judgment, and he shall be sworn in the same way as the others. Further, in all matters, the execution of which is entrusted to these twenty-five barons, if perchance these twenty-five are present and disagree about anything, or if some of them, after being summoned, are unwilling or unable to be present, that which the majority of those present ordain or command shall be held as fixed and established, exactly as if the whole twenty-five had concurred in this; and the said twenty-five shall swear that they will faithfully observe all that is aforesaid, and cause it to be observed with all their might. And we shall procure nothing from anyone, directly or indirectly, whereby any part of these concessions and liberties might be revoked or diminished; and if any such thing has been procured, let it be void and null, and we shall never use it personally or by another.

CHAPTER SIXTY-TWO

❴ Et omnes malas voluntates, indignaciones, et rancores ortos inter nos et homines nostros, clericos et laicos, a tempore discordie, plene omnibus remisimus et condonavimus. Preterea omnes transgressiones factas occasione ejusdem discordie, a Pascha anno regni nostri sextodecimo usque ad pacem reformatam, plene remisimus omnibus, clericis et laicis, et quantum ad nos pertinet plene condonavimus. Et insuper fecimus eis fieri litteras testimoniales patentes domini Stephani Cantuariensis archiepiscopi, domini Henrici Dublinensis archiepiscopi, et episcoporum predictorum, et magistri Pandulfi, super securitate ista et concessionibus prefatis.

And all the ill-will, hatreds, and bitterness that have arisen between us and our men, clergy and lay, from the date of the quarrel, we have completely remitted and pardoned to everyone. Moreover, all trespasses occasioned by the said quarrel, from Easter in the sixteenth year of our reign till the restoration of peace, we have fully remitted to all, both clergy and laymen, and completely forgiven, as far as pertains to us. And on this head, we have caused to be made for them letters testimonial patent of the lord Stephen, archbishop of Canterbury, of the lord Henry, archbishop of Dublin, of the bishops aforesaid, and of Master Pandulf as touching this security and the concessions aforesaid.

Appendix

CHAPTER SIXTY-THREE

❡ Quare volumus et firmiter precipimus quod Anglicana ecclesia libera sit et quod homines in regno nostro habeant et teneant omnes prefatas libertates, jura, et concessiones, bene et in pace, libere et quiete, plene et integre sibi et heredibus suis, de nobis et heredibus nostris, in omnibus rebus et locis, in perpetuum, sicut predictum est. Juratum est autem tam ex parte nostra quam ex parte baronum, quod hec omnia supradicta bona fide et sine malo ingenio observabuntur. Testibus supradictis et multis aliis. Data per manum nostram in prato quod vocatur Ronimede, inter Windlesoram et Stanes, quinto decimo die Junii, anno regni nostri decimo septimo.

Wherefore it is our will, and we firmly enjoin, that the English Church be free, and that the men in our kingdom have and hold all the aforesaid liberties, rights, and concessions, well and peaceably, freely and quietly, fully and wholly, for themselves and their heirs, of us and our heirs, in all respects and in all places forever, as is aforesaid. An oath, moreover, has been taken, as well on our part as on the part of the barons, that all these conditions aforesaid shall be kept in good faith and without evil intent. Given under our hand—the above-named and many others being witnesses—in the meadow which is called Runnymede, between Windsor and Staines, on the fifteenth day of June, in the seventeenth year of our reign.